An extract from

INVESTOR'S GUIDE

The Empowered Investor

Manage Your Investments the Way the Professionals Do

MARK HARRISON

Prentice Hall

FINANCIAL TIMES

An imprint of **Pearson Education**

London • New York • Toronto • Sydney • Tokyo • Singapore
Hong Kong • Cape Town • Madrid • Paris • Amsterdam • Munich • Milan

PEARSON EDUCATION LIMITED

Head Office:
Edinburgh Gate
Harlow CM20 2JE
Tel: +44 (0)1279 623623
Fax: +44 (0)1279 431059

London Office:
128 Long Acre
London WC2E 9AN
Tel: +44 (0)20 7447 2000
Fax: +44 (0)20 7447 2170
Website: www.financialminds.com

First published in Great Britain in 2002

© Mark Harrison 2002

The right of Mark Harrison to be identified as Author
of this Work has been asserted by him in accordance
with the Copyright, Designs and Patents Act 1988.

ISBN 0 273 65943 X

British Library Cataloguing in Publication Data
A CIP catalogue record for this book can be obtained from the British Library

10 9 8 7 6 5 4 3 2

Typeset by Northern Phototypesetting Co. Ltd, Bolton
Printed and bound in Great Britain by Clays Ltd

The Publishers' policy is to use paper manufactured from sustainable forests.

This publication is designed to provide accurate and authoritative information in regard to the subject
matter covered. It is sold with the understanding that neither the author nor the publisher is engaged in
rendering legal, investing, or any other professional service. If legal advice or other expert assistance is
required, the service of a competent professional person should be sought.

The publisher and contributors make no representation, express or implied, with regard to the accuracy
of the information contained in this book and cannot accept any responsibility or liability for any errors
or omissions that it may contain.

About the author

Mark Harrison joined www.iii.co.uk, the financial website, as Chief Investment Editor in 1999. In 2000 the site won the Bradford & Bingley Personal Finance New Media Site of the Year and in 2001 it won the Investors Chronicle Best Online Content Award.

Mark trained as a securities analyst at Credit Lyonnais Laing before spending three years as part of a team managing £20 billion of assets for Guardian Asset Management. Mark is a Member of the Association for Investment Management and Research in the US and an Associate of the UK Society of Investment Professionals. He was educated at Lincoln College, Oxford.

Foreword

With 2002 providing the third successive year of stock market falls in both the UK and the US, only confident, well informed investors have continued to trade.

However, as Barclays Capital's latest Equity Gilt study shows, equities remain the most attractive investment class over the longer term. According to data compiled since 1899, equities held over two years outperformed cash in 68 out of 102 years, while extending the holding period out to 10 years increases the probability of equity outperformance to 93%. This same data shows that since 1899, equities have presented a real return of 5.0%, compared with 1.2% for gilts and 1.0% for cash. In addition, income from dividends has once again become a key factor in investment decision making. The impact of dividend reinvestment is evident when comparing the value of £100 invested in 1899 when dividends are not reinvested (£142) compared to the resulting £14,847, when they are.

When we examine the cause of the extremes of the stockmarket's latest boom-to-bust we find much of it embedded in investor behaviour, with the herd mentality of the private investor leading to decisions to buy at the top and sell at the bottom. This book takes the private investor through the pitfalls of investing; aiming to provide the tools whereby the lessons of the past three years can be learned and benefited from. The efficient market hypothesis may decree that at any time the share price reflects all known information about a share price, but an investor may structure a portfolio to reflect their own risk profile and time horizon. It is vital to recognise the effect of 'noise' on share prices, while following share dealings by company directors can provide a valuable insight.

Technical analysis, or Chartism, features in Chapter 4. Technical analysis used to be largely ignored by City analysts, who dismissed the idea that it is possible to predict future share price movements from the past, as it is akin to driving while looking only in the rear view mirror. However, it is now increasingly recognized as a useful additional investment tool. Finally the book gives the private investor an insight into how to do their own research, concluding with a useful guide to on-line resources.

There is no doubt that investing in the stockmarket will remain challenging in this uncertain environment. However, both equities and bonds should remain a key part of any longer term investment portfolio, and with the help of this book we hope you will better be able to work out your optimal investment strategy.

Hilary Cook is a director for Barclays Investment Strategy and is a regular commentator in the financial press and on the television and radio. She is well-known for her practical and plain-speaking approach to market issues, to benefit the private investor.

Contents

NB Shaded sections indicate inclusion within this book

An extract from *The Empowered Investor* published by
Financial Times Prentice Hall © Mark Harrison

Preface

At the height of the boom in technology shares in 1999, one of the leading stockbrokers took a call from a client. 'I want to buy a thousand of whatever that bloke on the telly just tipped,' he said. 'Don't know the name of the share, just buy me a thousand shares quick.'[1] I haven't written the book for him since he may well be beyond hope. I have written it to help investors exploit the opportunities of the stockmarket, to realize the benefits of the latest technologies and to take intelligent decisions for themselves.

The technology stock boom has created many new investors. Some have been disappointed, but many have caught the bug. There has been a huge growth in trading, especially over the internet which now accounts for one in five trades in the UK. Equally many private investors have become disenchanted with the fund management industry, which has a habit of heavily promoting sectors just before a downturn.

These new active investors and traders are becoming a force to be reckoned with around the world as they already are in the USA. They want to be on equal terms with the institutions by having access to all the best information. 'They do not accept that there should be a charmed circle of brokers, analysts and institutional investors with privileged access to corporate data.'[2] Individual private investors now demand a level playing field to furnish them with enough independent information to take their own decisions.

My object in writing this book is to empower private investors to build and manage a portfolio of investments. Portfolio might seem a forbidding word suggesting ancient, leather-bound binders full of papers. Nothing could be further from the truth. If you have more than one share then you have a portfolio. Everyone can have a portfolio. With new technology you can manage it entirely without the burdens of accumulating piles of paper and expensive administration costs.

By your portfolio I don't mean your house, your pension and any cash you have for emergencies. Since your home is not real spendable stuff, you should not account for that in the same way as you do your shares. The same applies to your pension which, although a portfolio of assets, is designed to match a set of liabilities to provide for your retirement.

I am talking less about the selection of individual shares, but rather about the deliberate combination of shares into a portfolio. To do this you can learn to use all the tools of the fund managers' trade and to think just how the professionals think. I have at one time or another been a stockbroking analyst, part of a team managing a £20 billion institutional fund and a financial journalist so I suppose I have been around the block and back. One thing is certain: no professional investor would invest a penny on the back of a tip he saw on TV.

There is a world of difference between a tip and an analysis. For a start, analysts are regulated for the protection of investors and journalists are not. Analysts cannot 'front run' or buy shares for themselves before tipping them. If they do then they risk losing their licence to practise and damaging the reputation of their firm. No such binding restrictions apply to journalists. A tip in a newspaper could be a one-liner made up in the bath. It could be founded on nothing more substantial than the fact that it sounds clever. Analysts who are, as I am, members of professional bodies are bound to have a reasonable and objective basis for their conclusions.

So how do analysts analyze? The results of a survey of 185 US investment managers and bankers are shown below. Fundamental analysis and technical analysis are clear favourites. But we shall look at all three in turn.

Favourite professional techniques of investing[3]

Fundamental analysis	74 per cent
Portfolio analysis	30 per cent
Technical analysis	35 per cent

I feel that the best place to start is by first exposing the way information flows about the stockmarket. The next step will be to examine ways to profit from inefficiencies in the flow of information. Then we can journey through the professional toolkits of fundamental and technical analysis. After that we will be ready to tear apart the myth that building a winning portfolio is the preserve of investment managers. Finally, we can learn something from how investors such as John Maynard Keynes, Warren Buffett and Jim Slater mastered their age and achieved fortunes through investing in both bull and bear markets. For your entertainment and instruction I have also included a few pages on the great bubbles and crashes.

Acknowledgments

Just to prove I didn't write all this off the top of my head, I should like to credit Fred Wellings for his acute analyst-training seminars at Crédit Lyonnais Securities, the Association for Investment Management and Research whose CFA program helped organize my thoughts on portfolio analysis, and the many users of iii, the financial website, particularly during that brief spring of 2000 when it seemed we had discovered a new eternal truth and shaken old prejudices. Robert Barrie of Credit Suisse First Boston, Clyde Lewis and Julian Marshall of HSBC Securities, Anil Raval at Ample Interactive Investor, Tom Stevenson at Hemscott.net, staff at the UKSIP, City Business and Guildhall Libraries and the custodians of the Keynes literary estate all win mentions for promptly dealing with my queries. Rafael Gómes Rodriguez reminded me that simple English words are always best. Jonathan Agbenyega and Richard Stagg, my publishers, showed commendable faith in the appetite for knowledge of private investors. I owe grateful thanks to Penelope Allport for unflappingly managing this project through production and to Susan G. R. Williams for accurate and vigilant proofing.

Enjoy the book and best of luck in your investing.

Mark A. Harrison
Clerkenwell, London
December 2001

NOTES

1 Justin Urquhart Stewart of 7 Investment Management, a division of Killik & Co.
2 Howard Davies, Chairman of the Financial Services Authority, in a speech to the Investor Relations Institute, 9 July 2001.
3 R. C. Carter and H. Van Auken, 'Security analysis and portfolio management: a survey and analysis', *Journal of Portfolio Management*, Spring (1990), p. 82.

1

The information wheel

I'd be a bum on the street with a tin cup if the markets were efficient. (Warren Buffett)[1]

I have noticed that everyone who ever told me that the markets are efficient is poor. (Larry Hite)[2]

Not long ago information flowed smoothly around the small, clubby world of the City of London. News about takeovers, profitability, new products or management incompetence was divided among a small circle of perhaps a couple of thousand brokers and fund managers on a daily basis.

The London Stock Exchange motto, 'My Word is My Bond', was to a large extent true and anyone who dared to break the rule was unceremoniously exiled. This world was brought to an end by liberalization of the ownership rules of the London Stock Exchange in the late 1980s. This 'Big Bang' prompted a rash of wheeling and dealing by US and overseas banks to buy up the European financial capital.

There is still an interdependent clubbiness in the City, of mutual favours and informal contracts. Companies who want to raise loans or issue shares have to rely on investment banks. For example, an investment bank will guarantee (or underwrite) the success of a rights issue, where a company sells its stock to existing stockholders, charging a fee of up to 15 per cent. In turn the investment bank will pass on the risk that stock may not be sold to sub-underwriters, often the investment managers who already own the stock. Again a fee changes hands.

Investment banks rely on investment managers to buy their loans and stocks and all rely on analysts and salesmen to convey and interpret information. A large investment bank will have not only a corporate department but also analysts, a stockbroking and an investment management arm.

JUMP ONTO THE INFORMATION WHEEL

The stock market can be thought of as a gigantic information-processing machine. Information will make or break your investment: information not so much about the past as about the future earning power of a stock. With a computer terminal we can now see prices reflecting almost instantly whatever is happening in the most distant corners of the world. When there is a legal ruling against a tobacco manufacturer in Los Angeles, the prices of tobacco makers around the globe reverberate. If there is an explosion in a refinery in Brazil, the share price of speciality chemical manufacturers of the product in England who will gain from the misfortune are instantly marked higher.

It is important to distinguish between stale information and new information. Past information is already impounded in the price of a stock. New information about future growth feeds change in the share price. Informed by our own information and analysis, millions of investors continuously vote as if in a gigantic opinion poll where the result is the market price of a stock. When new information appears there is a scramble to profit from it and the price adjusts to a new equilibrium.

> It is important to distinguish between stale information and new information.

So the stock market is a kind of competition among investors for the very best information. If there is no new information then the stock market will become stagnant. Then as pulses of new information appear, their energy will be consumed to fuel change in the market.

Better information allows superior analysis and higher profits from the anomalies between the market price and potential price you foresee. By your own buying or selling you will remove the opportunities for the less perceptive to arbitrage a profit for themselves as you and others rush to drive prices to the point where profitable opportunities do not exist.

This is not so much of a zero sum game as a positive sum game because the trend of earnings and prices is generally upwards. Other things being equal, company profits and stock prices will trend up with general economic growth. But that does not make it any easier to select stocks. In order to arrive at an investment decision to buy and sell you need to build up a mosaic of information to give you the confidence to do so.

If you look at fundamental information you may have been following company announcements, bulletin boards or economic indicators. If you are interested in charts, you could well have noticed a pattern or a trend.

Whichever way you invest, you will have acquainted yourself with significant facts. You will be able to give concrete reasons if someone asks you why you did the deal.

THE INFORMATION CHASE

Where does information come from and what is important? Information is not the same as market gossip. Information is what really determines the true or intrinsic value of a stock. It says something significant about the future earnings power of a stock. When as an analyst I talk about intrinsic value or economic value I am thinking of something entirely different to market value. A market value can be unduly influenced by the day-to-day fluctuations in the liquidity of a stock. For example, when an institution sells a large line of stock, the market price jumps about all over the place, whereas a theoretical value will be more stable. A small illiquid stock can be severely damaged by the attempt of a large shareholder to sell up, even if they are selling for some genuine technical reason.

Intrinsic value is unaffected by such short-term consideration and can be calculated yourself or taken from independent experts such as investment analysts. In fact anyone can calculate the theoretical value of a company. You can use ratios from accounting information, look at the quality of management, scrutinize market share or do your own assessment of a company's products. If you are mathematically inclined you can calculate a present value of future cash flows, though that is beyond the scope of this book.

There are really two families of information opportunities available for investors to exploit. The first is under-reaction and the second is over-reaction. Good news can lead to over-reaction. In which case you can profit by selling. But if news is good, prices may under react and then keep trending up and develop momentum. Momentum, where the price just keeps on going in one direction, is a longer term consequence of the price under-reacting to news in the short term.[3]

> There are two families of information opportunities available for investors to exploit. The first is under-reaction and the second is over-reaction.

All these sorts of news announcements provide measurable changes in value. Imagine a world where stock prices changed instantaneously in response to information alone rather than to market noise. In such a world prices would move up and down in giant leaps as soon as news was announced through the regulated channels. Active trading makes these leaps less pronounced and makes the stock market a lively and liquid place to trade.

There is one difficult notion that we are going to have to get out of the way first. This is the notion of markets being efficient. When the investment experts and academics talk about efficiency they don't mean quite the same thing as ordinary folk. We might think our new car is very efficient in doing 50 miles to the gallon when our neighbour's car does only 30 miles. Stock market efficiency is a little different. It is all about the way stock prices absorb news and adjust to it. If stock prices always reflect all the available information then they are always right, they are always efficient. But as we all can guess this is an unrealistic and rather academic theory. I don't know what it is about academics, but they always seem to take extreme positions and occupy opposite poles. In one corner these efficient marketeers hypothesize that market prices are supposed to adjust to all publicly available information on its release instantaneously preventing any possible trading opportunities. They call this the *Efficient Markets Hypothesis (EMH)*.[4]

EMH is in turn based on the more primitive idea that people behave rationally at all times to maximize their own benefit or utility and are able to process new information correctly. The argument of this book is that for one reason or another they basically do not, and I am in good company. According to George Soros, a speculator of some note: 'The theory [of efficient markets] is manifestly false – I have disproved it by consistently outperforming the averages.'[5] Soros believes that participants themselves distort the efficiency of markets by reacting to information in unexpected ways: 'Nothing could be further removed from reality than the assumption that participants base their decisions on perfect knowledge. People are groping to anticipate the future with the help of whatever guideposts they can establish.'[6]

What is the Efficient Markets Hypothesis? In a perfectly efficient market, prices are held to adjust to all publicly available information on its release instantaneously preventing any possible arbitrage trading opportunities.

NEW INFORMATION ON THE WHEEL

In the modern stock market, new information about companies first flows out from the company around a tightly knit circle of analysts, journalists, public relations and investor relations firms and finally to institutional and smaller investors (Figure 1.1).

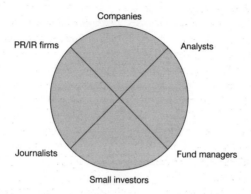

Figure 1.1 New information on the wheel

New information such as the figures on the sales of a new product first has to get through the company's management structure. You can easily imagine the product being introduced on your local high street and thousands of other high streets around the world. It may take time for a company to know whether the product is selling well in one region or another. They may have manufactured too much stock or have faulty products recalled. In a large company with many management layers, managers may disguise the failure of products from their bosses perhaps until after a bonus appraisal. Eventually the information will percolate to the office of the chief executive and a decision will be taken on whether the information is price sensitive and how and when to release the information to the outside world.

All major news announcements such as results, mergers, acquisitions or new contracts have to flow through formal stock exchange channels. In the UK this is the London Stock Exchange Regulatory News Service (RNS), while in the USA the official channel is the Securities and Exchange

Commission (SEC). They contain what is described as material non-public information. This is news that will likely influence the share price when it becomes known. These news announcements are simultaneously delivered as press releases to journalists and investors. On the day of announcements the managers of the company make themselves available first to investors (usually in order of size), then to securities analysts and lastly to journalists.

These formal channels are only the tip of the information iceberg. Firms of investor relations have grown up to provide a far more informal means of information flow. They arrange company visits for analysts and investors and massage expectations between the news announcements. While journalists and company managers have been around for centuries, analysts are a relatively young profession. In the USA they developed on Wall Street in the 1920s, often as statistical departments of stockbroking firms. In London they arrived in the 1960s and have expanded in number as stockbrokers and investment banks have merged. More recently investment management companies have developed their own analyst departments. The job of a securities analyst is basically to form and communicate investment recommendations to their clients or employers.

Because of their close access to institutional investors and influence on public opinion, analysts are given privileged access to companies and company managers. They are given 'clues' as to how the companies are faring. Increasingly companies have been under pressure to provide equal access to new information and to appear transparent. The distribution power of the internet has made instant simultaneous information distribution easy. But there remain marked differences in the information that companies make available on their eponymous corporate websites.

There are seasonal patterns for news flow with lots of announcements after the end of the tax year. Bad news often flows out when markets are shut or on a Friday after the close of trade. Takeover news also has a tendency to develop over the weekend, described in the trade as the 'Friday night drop'. When markets are shut, foreign markets can reflect market sentiment through foreign listings which most large companies maintain abroad.

HOW CAN THE INDIVIDUAL PRIVATE INVESTOR BEAT THE PROFESSIONALS?

With thousands of analysts and professionals scouring the market for bargains every day, you might think that there are not many overlooked opportunities around to exploit: 'The more skillful analysts there are, the harder it will be for the average practitioner to "beat the market".'[7] Even the fund managers are complaining. For professional fund managers at the giant fund management firms, it is hard work to find profitable information and getting harder still as their funds grow. With competition for information becoming ever more intense, professionals have a tough time in trying to outperform one another. According to one: 'We could not beat the market because we were rapidly becoming the market.'[8]

INDIVIDUAL PRIVATE INVESTORS CAN BEAT THE MARKET

- Understand your own investing behaviour – know the great bubbles, understand overconfidence, overtrading and misleading frameworks.
- Understand the investing behaviour of the professionals – learn from the master investors.
- Jump on the information wheel – know when you have spotted really new information.
- Know the market anomalies – growth stocks, small firms effect, ratios effects, calendar effects.
- Build a winning, balanced portfolio using professional tools – broker research, online information, screens and online portfolios.

Understanding your investing behaviour

The diversity of our opinions does not proceed from some being more rational than others but solely from the fact that our thoughts pass through diverse channels and the same objects are not considered by all. (Rene Déscartes)[9]

How is it that with equal access to the same information two investors will probably come up with completely different conclusions? In recent years a rather frighteningly named group of theorists, Behaviouralists, have been trying to find patterns in such things. What they suggest is that people behave in predictable ways in their investing and that these explain the way share prices move. Behaviouralists are basically taking commonly observed patterns such as avarice, aversion to risk, impatience and the formation of habits and slapping categories on top of them. Once we have got to grips with a couple of these categories, then we will be better able to spot shares that are trading at the wrong market price.

> Behaviouralists are basically taking commonly observed patterns such as avarice, aversion to risk, impatience and the formation of habits and slapping categories on top of them.

Professional investors live in a rather more rarefied world. They have the experience and the time to allocate all their resources to working out how particular stock prices will respond to the various categories of information. Private investors are less well informed and have less time. There is always the temptation to oversimplify, reducing investment into a couple of investment techniques and maxims such as: 'Always invest when directors are buying their own shares or when the P/E ratio is low.' While these are both sound principles it is advisable to study the detail before relying on a rule. We shall look at behavioural finance in some more detail later.

> **What is a P/E ratio?** This is the price per share divided by the earnings per share, i.e. if price is 100 and earnings are 10 the P/E is 10. So you are paying up ten years of today's earnings if you buy it.

Markets are not efficient

Find out the inefficiencies and profit from them

Between the autumn of 1929 and 8 July 1932 the US stock market lost over 90 per cent of its value. It didn't all happen in one go, although it had a violent beginning. On Thursday 24 October, the first day of the crash, a syndicate headed by Mr J.P. Morgan and executed by Richard Whitney thought it was getting a bargain when it bought US Steel stock at 205. They had recently traded as high as 258 that very summer. By 5 November 1929, US Steel was 165. On 8 July 1932, US Steel was trading at only 22. Doesn't look like the price was very efficient in reflecting anything other than the panic of those years.

Why were stock prices in London 11 per cent less valuable on one particular day, 19 October 1987, than they were the day before? Can it happen again? The huge change in prices from one day to the next is pretty good evidence that prices are not really that efficient. They sometimes respond not to new information, proper news, but rather to noise and dealings. Some would argue that the irrational influences would cancel each other out, but markets do not seem to be as efficient in pricing stocks as we might hope.

Following directly from this is the useful suggestion that we can hope to find predictable aspects of inefficiency. If you can find out where and why the market is not effective at pricing in information then you can profit from the anomalies. According to the experts who (unsurprisingly) have been swarming to discover the market's secrets for the last fifty years, here they are:

> If you can find out where and why the market is not effective at pricing in information then you can profit from the anomalies.

1. Buy growth stocks.
2. Buy smaller companies.
3. Watch your ratios (low P/E and low Price/Book).
4. Watch the pros.
5. Timing effects.
6. Check out the investment announcements.
7. Beat the index trackers at their own game.

You may be familiar with some of these successful strategies from your own investing, but it is always nice to be proven right and have some concrete evidence provided by experts.

BUY COMPANIES FORECASTING GROWTH

Should we buy growth stocks – after all they have already gone up? Earnings announcements are really central to the valuation of companies. They convey information about current and future prospects. This is where expectations and reality about growth coincide. Prior to the release of earnings, the market will have built up expectations on the likely figure represented in the *consensus earnings forecast*. The magnitude of the reaction is determined by the extent to which earnings meet investors' expectations. Undershoot expectations and your share price may promptly nosedive.

What is the consensus earnings forecast? This is just the average forecast of all the stockbroking analysts of the earnings of a company in the coming year. If there are only two brokers, one forecasting 10p and the other 20p, the consensus will be 15p.

Investors look to the *earnings per share (EPS)* as the key information output and the main measure of past and future growth. Growth is important and becoming more so in a world where inflation is low. Because EPS is an input into the other key ratio used by investors, P/E, its importance to investors cannot be exaggerated. Of course general information about the economy, the firm's markets and products will be widely available long before the release of final results and annual reports. There will be reports from competitor firms, management announcements and the interim report to provide updates in between. So wide-awake observers like the analysts can guesstimate future earnings changes.

One study by academics of the link between earnings and price returns found that the market price of shares does anticipate the direction of reported announcements on profits. According to this around 80 per cent of the attributable price change comes before the release of the annual report and 20 per cent after.[10] One explanation of market under-reaction on the release of announcements is that old habits die hard. Confronted with new information about a company, investors have to relate it to their existing views. They tend not to react as much as the information warrants because of their instinctive conservatism. At the same time, when investors are bombarded with good news they not only drop their old conservatism, but adopt a frame of mind that underestimates the possibility of failure.[11]

> Investors look to the *earnings per share (EPS)* as the key information output and the main measure of past and future growth.

The implications are that we should pay up for growth particularly if we spot a positive change in the trend of announcements. The fact that the share price anticipates the direction and amount of earnings is key evidence against the theory of perfectly efficient markets since, according to that, price changes should occur only after the release of results and not a moment before.

BUY SMALL FIRMS

Another major opportunity is the fact that smaller firms tend to outperform the market even when returns are adjusted for risk. This suggests that investing in a portfolio of smaller sized firms is a good investment strategy. Six good reasons to buy small firms are as follows:

1. Profits and dividend growth can be faster than with larger companies because they are starting from a lower base.
2. There are no bureaucracies to stifle bright ideas in small companies.
3. They are small and nimble enough to adapt flexibly to fast-changing market conditions.
4. Over the long term, studies show a premium over normal returns of 8–17 per cent, persisting over long periods and after transaction costs in many countries.[12] You could have had an extra $1m if you had invested $1000 in smaller rather than larger US companies in 1926 and let the money grow to 2000.
5. Good small companies may fall below the radar screens of the big investors and analyst coverage is shallow, resulting in many neglected opportunities.
6. Takeover activity is likely to be more common in smaller companies.

There are several possible explanations which confirm that small companies are fertile hunting grounds for bargains. One is that the costs of investing in smaller stocks are higher due to wide dealing spreads, so you would expect returns to be better. However, the magnitude of the premium over normal returns is so large (8–17 per cent) that transaction costs from wide bid/ask spreads are dwarfed.

Another explanation argues that smaller firms are more risky and that the return is merely compensation for risk that is difficult to compute. But even adjusting for risk, returns from smaller companies are still abnormally large. Another possible explanation focuses on the neglect of some companies by analysts. This results in poor availability of high quality information. It is common sense that if you have less information you can demand a higher return.

WATCH YOUR RATIOS

Buy on low P/Es

If you remember nothing else about P/E ratios, remember to avoid stocks with excessively high ones. You'll save yourself a lot of money if you do. With few exceptions, an extremely high P/E ratio is a handicap to a stock, in the same way that extra weight in the saddle is a handicap to a racehorse. (Peter Lynch)[13]

Many investors use P/Es and nothing else because they are easy to calculate and allow stocks to be quickly compared. But to my mind there is there is no right or wrong P/E. When you do the calculation of dividing price by earnings per share, you just get a number that is a starting point to work with. The more you know about the individual company, the less informative it is. You can use past earnings or more realistically you can use future earnings to calculate the ratio. But you must be sure to be comparing like with like.

Looking at the whole market over time, P/Es are up and down like a yo-yo. Take the US stockmarket. Since 1926 the P/E has averaged 14.4 and ranged from a low of 5.9 in 1949 to a high of 35 in 1999. A dollar of earnings could be worth $5.9 a share or $35.[14] This is a wide disparity. In the early 1970s stock prices of a group of large companies known as the Nifty Fifty, which included Sony Corporation and McDonald's, traded at 60–90 times earnings. At this time the market as a whole had a P/E of 18. In 1961 the P/E had risen from its post-war low to 22 and then fell down to 7 in 1980 before accelerating to its recent high of 35. Which one was the right level? The answer is that they all seemed pretty right to investors buying stocks on the day.

Buying low P/E stocks is one of the oldest ways of discriminating in favour of stocks. The idea is that stocks with a low P/E or conversely high earnings to price are likely to be undervalued and earn future excess returns. Benjamin Graham, the founder of modern security analysis, used P/E ratios as a screen to identify undervalued stocks in his classic, *Security Analysis: Principals and Techniques* (1934). The performance figures seem to back him up. From 1967 to 1988, US firms in the lowest P/E decile earned an average return of 16.26 per cent, while those with the highest P/E ratios earned only 6.64 per cent. These excess returns are mimicked worldwide.[15]

> Buying low P/E stocks is one of the oldest ways of discriminating in favour of stocks.

The excess returns from stocks with low P/E ratios cannot be explained as a compensation for extra risk because most low P/E stocks have low growth, large size, high assets and stable businesses. These are characteristics of dull and safe businesses that diminish risk. Obviously a rule of buying on the basis of a low P/E excludes many companies of merit that are not yet in profit or whose earnings have been disrupted by cycles or corporate events.

The other problem with investing on the basis of low P/Es is what is known as 'aggressive accounting', where companies deliberately adopt an accounting practice to flatter their earnings. Other perfectly proper accounting practices distort earnings such as by restructuring charges or the amortization of goodwill. Overall buying on P/E ratios sounds like a pretty good bet providing you check out the company and its earnings in more detail.

Buy low Price/Book

> It is not size that counts in business. Some companies with $500,000 capital are making more profits than other companies with $5,000,000. Size is a handicap unless efficiency goes with it. (Herbert N. Casson)[16]

If you take a look at the balance sheet in the accounts of any company, you will see that there is a line called shareholders' funds or equity. This is what is known as *book value* (BV). It is not money that shareholders can have back if they ask politely; nor is it money that the company can splash out on anything it likes.

Book value is exactly what it says, just the value in the company's book of its net assets. The true value may be lower because an asset such as machinery has worn out, or higher because land or technology has gone up in value. The ratio of price to book is simply the price per share divided by book value per share. The price to book anomaly captures the outperformance of firms whose underlying assets are a high proportion (or even larger) of the market value. So you buy low Price/Book and sell high Price/Book.

> **B**ook value is exactly what it says, just the value in the company's book of its net assets.

Book value is always a fairly stable number. It will not chop and change as much as earnings and high book value will be a characteristic of relatively low risk firms.

Table 1.1	Excess annual returns of low Price/Book stocks, 1981–92[17]

	%
France	3.26
Germany	1.39
UK	1.09
USA	1.06

Source: Asweth Damodaran (1996) *Investment Valuation*, New York: Wiley, p. 177.

What is Price to Book (P/BV)? This is simply the price per share divided by the book value per share or the shareholders' funds divided by the total market capitalization. If the price is 100 and the book value is also 100 the P/BV is 1.

Information on book value can be found in the annual report of a company. A bank may have a Price/BV of around one while an industrial company would be more likely to be greater than one. But because book value is calculated on the basis of historical cost of the assets, an industrial company may overstate the true value of worn-out machinery.

Benjamin Graham used P/BV to select stocks and was particularly keen on stocks with P/BVs above two-thirds, i.e. more than two-thirds of the share price could be covered by book asset value. While this may have helped Graham to avoid investing in too many duds during the Great American Depression, it seems a conservative strategy in a time of low inflation and more professionally managed economies. We should not forget that assets attract maintenance and upkeep expenditure for their owners.

Buying low Price/Book stocks seems a winning strategy since you are investing in mostly stable and low risk stocks. But it is probably a good idea to check out that all the book assets in which you are investing are actually producing cash flow. Double-check that the dividends are covered and not a relic of some bygone era of prosperity.

WATCH THE PROS

Buy on insider-director dealings and fund manager trades

> With enough inside information and a million dollars you can go broke in a year. (Warren Buffett)[18]

A whole industry has grown around tracking director and institutional dealings. The reasoning for this is that directors and large institutional shareholders are privy to important private information, or at the very least able to react to public information before the rest of us have the chance. Fortunately in most countries such trades have to be reported to the local stock exchange. In the USA, corporate insiders, as they are called, have to report their transactions in their employer's shares to the SEC each month. In the UK director's dealings and share trades by holders of more than 3 per cent of an issue are reported as soon as practicable. So we can monitor the trends in these purchases or sales.

With director's dealings we are just seeing the tip of the iceberg. There are all manner of reasons why a director may be buying. They may be exercising a stock option; they may just have been appointed and want to demonstrate commitment to their new employer; they may be making a minor adjustment to a huge shareholding. But the evidence is that corporate insiders consistently enjoy above average returns, especially on purchase transactions.[19] It seems that transactions by the chairman and CEO are the most useful to follow. Because of investor interest in these data the *Wall Street Journal* in the USA and the *Financial Times* in the UK publish columns discussing the largest insider trades.

I must admit that this is one of my favourite strategies other than buying small firms. I always check what the directors are doing and I suspect that sometimes they use their dealings to signal to the market. Occasionally they may attempt to send out false signals. I find the fund manager dealings less useful, except in some smaller companies where the presence of a good fund manager can also prompt his following to buy.

Buy or sell on analyst recommendations

Analysts operate at the core of a matrix of information flow between the companies they analyze and the stock market. They use both publicly available and private information to formulate and issue buy and sell recommendations. As you might expect, there is evidence that both buy and sell recommendations affect the prices of stocks (Figure 1.2).

Analysts have come in for a lot of flak recently. The problem is that analysts are part of giant investment banks with both corporate financing and analyst departments divided by 'Chinese walls'. The suspicion is that they are not immune to pressures from elsewhere in their institution, which may be a sizeable shareholder in the company being analyzed or may have a corporate finance relationship. It turns out that only about 3 per cent of analyst recommendations lately have been sells. In their favour, analysts are anxious to be seen as independent and there are moves afoot to restore the reputation of analysts and their employers.[20]

Another allied issue is the *analyst neglect effect* that it is believed to contribute to the low valuation of many smaller companies. The fewer the number of analysts covering a stock, then the bigger the adjustment when new information finally appears.

Back the fund managers?

If markets were perfectly efficient, then there would be no need for fund managers to chop and change their portfolios to try and outperform the index. Stockmarket prices would always fully reflect the available information and outperformance would be impossible. So in an efficient market you might as well buy an index fund.

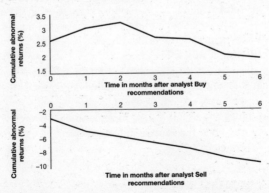

Figure 1.2 **Share prices respond to analyst Sell recommendations more than Buy recommendations**

Source: 'Do Stockbroking Analysts Earn Their Bonuses?', *Professional Investor*, May 2001, p. 16. With permission of UKSIP

You would think that, if there were any market anomalies to take advantage of, money managers would be in a better position than most to exploit them. However the facts are that by and large they do not outperform. One famous study by Jensen[21] showed that of 115 fund managers, only 26 outperformed the market. But this is not overwhelming evidence of efficient markets because in a truly efficient market no funds at all should be able to outperform.

Gurus and investment systems

The obvious follow-on from looking at analyst recommendations is to identify some analytical techniques that are better than others. In the USA, studies have been done on Value Line to test this. Value Line is a large financial information advisory service that has built a model with four elements to it – a four-factor formula model. This divides around 1700 common stocks into five ranked groups. The model assigns weights based on the four factors:

- P/E relative to other companies
- price momentum
- year-on-year earnings changes
- the difference between actual and forecast earnings (earnings surprise).

The results are illustrated in Figure 1.3. One study shows that the top ranked group in this model outperforms the bottom ranked group by 20

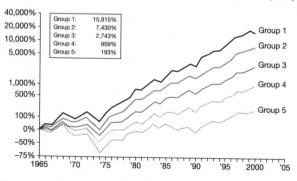

Figure 1.3   **The success of Value Line's stock selections**

Source: 'Value Line outperforms the DOW® by 20 to 1', **www.valueline.com** July 2000. Reproduced with permission of Value Line Inc, 220 East 42nd Street, New York, NY 10017

per cent.[22] However, Value Line's own Centurion Fund, which invests in stocks in the top-ranked Value Line group, has underperformed consistently over the past decade.

Spot the dodgy system!

Watch out for:

- transaction costs – which can eat away profits.
- survivors' bias, where stocks that go bankrupt are screened out to leave only the winners.
- misleading graph scales showing the results.
- size of the universe of data – is it so big it could prove almost anything?
- whether the system claims credit for the successful strategy of yesteryear.
- whether the assumptions of the system are fully disclosed.

Surveys of equities analysts by Womack in the USA and AQ in the UK are similarly inconclusive. There is rarely evidence of consistent success by an individual analyst. Womack does however find greater accuracy in regard to sell recommendations than buy recommendations. Even if an analyst is inaccurate, this is not to say that they are not influential. So it is worth finding out who are the most influential analysts in surveys of analyst rankings according to fund managers and companies analyzed. These are produced annually as the Reuters Surveys and also by Extel.

TIMING EFFECTS

Another oddity is the tendency for markets to perform well during the first month of the tax year. This is because investors engage in selling to establish their liability to tax at the end of the tax year. After New Year there is a rush to re-acquire those stocks that look attractive. So if you buy stocks in the last month of the tax year you should beat the market.[23] There is also evidence of a weekend effect where market prices tend to open at lower levels on a Monday than they closed the previous Friday.[24]

BUY ON INVESTMENT ANNOUNCEMENTS

Many people think that a surefire way to make money is to buy on news announcements, but this is more of an art than a mechanical science. You have to ask yourself, 'What informational advantage do we have over other traders?'[25] Intuitively we can guess that if a firm invests in something, then there is a possibility that the project will succeed. If we own the stock the day before the announcement of new investment, we can rightly demand that, if we sell that stock the day after, it reflects a premium for the possibility of the new project succeeding.

There is evidence that joint venture formations, expenditure on research and development and capital expenditure projects all have an appreciable effect on share prices (around +1.5 per cent in the month of the announcement).

BEAT THE INDEX TRACKERS AT THEIR OWN GAME

An increasing percentage of the market is now controlled by index funds, which mechanically invest in all the constituents of the chosen index without any input from analysts or fund managers. By and large these do the job they are supposed to do – one study reports the earliest US index funds have tracked the S&P 500 with a correlation of 98 per cent. From zero in 1971, when Wells Fargo set up the first index tracker, the amount involved in index funds exceeded $1 trillion a few years ago.

What this means is that a large sector of the market is investing in the success or failure of one particular index. Stocks outside the index or stocks moving in and out may find themselves undervalued or overvalued purely because of the buying and selling by index trackers to keep up with the index. This creates obvious arbitrage opportunities for investors keeping an eye on stocks at the fringes of indices. Since fund managers are paid to outperform the indices, many have basically given up stockpicking and in reality keep their funds closely matched to the benchmark index. This is referred to as informal or 'closet' index tracking.

An example of the absurd situation that both formal index tracking and informal index tracking can produce was when the UK's Vodafone merged with a large US operator, Airtouch, instantly increasing its techni-cal weight in the index. According to one fund manager, 'I'm surrounded by people who are all buying Vodafone in the wake of the Airtouch announcement. We all think it is expensive, but we've got to buy it to maintain our weight in the sector. The more we buy it, the more the price rises, so we have to buy more.'[26]

SUMMARY AND CONCLUSION

The arbs

We are not the only people to know about these anomalies and inefficien-cies. There are thousands of hedge funds around the world that can also borrow money to invest in market inefficiencies. In a perfectly efficient market these arbitrageurs would ensure that all opportunities for a quick profit were instantly arbitraged away. However, the arbs (short for arbi-trageurs) cannot know everything and it will always take time for them to catch on. There is often difficulty in effectively and cheaply shorting stock. Shorting is selling stock you do not own in the hope you can deliver it in settlement by buying it back at a cheaper price in the future. (Don't worry if you can't get your head around shorting or arbitrage – you are not alone.) Then there is the problem of finding substitutes to exercise an arbi-trage between two like but mispriced assets.

There are currently over 2000 US hedge funds worth about $175bn and thousands more elsewhere.[27] Occasionally they go bust. In August and September 1998 it emerged that Long Term Capital Management (LTCM), a fund known for its large size, high leverage and the employment of the Nobel Prize winning academics Myron Scholes and Robert Merton, lost nearly half of its $3–4bn of equity. The default of Russia on its debt had triggered a market collapse that floored LTCM and several other hedge funds. A rescue of LTCM was then coordinated by the Federal Reserve Bank of New York, an intervention justified by Alan Greenspan, Chair-man of the Fed, in these terms: 'A fire sale may be sufficiently intense and widespread that it seriously distorts markets and elevates uncertainty enough to impair the overall functioning of the economy.' In other words the financial system had been brought to the brink of collapse.

One other problem involving arbitrage is that mispricings which should not be there just are – and persist for long periods of time. For example, many investment trusts in the UK and closed end funds in the USA trade at very different values to their underlying assets for long periods of time. Royal Dutch and Shell are independently listed in the Netherlands and the UK. This is a structure that grew out of an agreement in 1907 between Royal Dutch and Shell by which the two companies merged while retaining their separate lists, on a 60:40 basis. Royal Dutch got 60 per cent of cash flows and Shell got 40 per cent. So in theory Royal Dutch should trade at 1.5 times Shell. In fact there are enormous deviations from this theoretical value that persist over long periods. If markets were truly rational and efficient, such problems would not arise. There would be no profits for arbitrageurs to arbitrage away.

To my mind all of these, particularly the outperformance of small firms, ratios effects and analyst recommendations, are compelling evidence against efficient markets. The last irony is that there is evidence that the market may be getting more inefficient because those who believe in efficient markets are investing in index funds, which distort the share prices of many stocks.

NOTES

1 Janet C. Lowe, *Warren Buffett Speaks: Wit and Wisdom from the World's Greatest Investor* (Wiley, New York, 1997), p. 93.
2 Attributed to Larry Hite, Mint Investment Management Company.
3 Andrei Shleifer, *Inefficient Markets* (Oxford University Press, Oxford, 2000), p. 18.
4 The framework of efficient markets theory is that prices are the sum of all available information and seamlessly adjust to all new information instantly. This can be thought of as a formal academic model. You have your inputs of various kinds of information and then you have your outputs in that prices respond measurably. It was in fact an academic physicist, Eugene Fama, who tied this together as the Efficient Markets Hypothesis (EMH). Fama classifies information into three sets corresponding to a weak, semi-strong and strong form of EMH. The first is an information set that includes only the past stock price information. This implies that past prices cannot be useful in any shape or form in predicting future prices. Technical analysis, which arrives at chart patterns and trends from past price data, is consequently a waste of time. We shall explore some of the evidence against this later. The second set of information is all publicly available information such as company accounts and government statistics. According to EMH, this is instantly reflected in the price as soon as it is known. Fundamental analysis is thus a waste of time. The final set of information includes all public and privately held information. This would include secret takeover talks and the like. Prosecutions against insider dealers such as Ivan Boesky are evidence against the last set of information.

5   George Soros, *The Alchemy of Finance* (Simon and Schuster, New York, 1987), p. 47.

6   George Soros, *The Alchemy of Finance* (Simon and Schuster, New York, 1987), p. 45.

7   Peter Bernstein, *Capital Ideas* (Free Press, New York, 1993), p. 161.

8   Peter Bernstein, *Capital Ideas* (Free Press, New York, 1993), p. 140.

9   Rene Déscartes, 'Discourse on the method of rightly conducting the reason', in *The Great Books of the Western World: Déscartes and Spinoza* (Franklin Library, Franklin Centre, PA, 1982), p. 69.

10 Ray Ball and Philip Brown, 'An empirical evaluation of accounting numbers', *Journal of Accounting Research*, autumn (1968), pp. 159–78.

11 Andrei Shleifer, *Inefficient Markets* (Oxford University Press, Oxford, 2000), p. 112.

12 In the USA, R.W. Banz, 'The relationship between return and market values of common stocks', *Journal of Financial Economics*, 9, 1 (1981). p. 3–18. Marc Reinganum, 'Misspecification of capital asset pricing', *Journal of Financial Economics*, 9, 1 (1981), pp. 19–46. In the UK, Dimson and Marsh 1955–84 found outperformance of 7 per cent. For France, Bergstrom, Frashure and Chisholm reported a premium of 8.8 per cent over the period 1975–89 and a slightly smaller effect in Germany. Hameo 1989 reported a small firm premium of 5.1 per cent for Japanese stocks between 1971 and 1988.

13 Peter Lynch, *One Up on Wall Street* (Simon and Schuster, New York, 2000), p. 165.

14 C. Barry White, 'What P/E will the US market support?', *Financial Analysts Journal*, 56, 6 (2000), p. 30.

15 Asweth Damodaran, *Investment Valuation* (Wiley, New York, 1996), p. 175–6.

16 Dean LeBaron and Romesh Vaitilingam with Marilyn Pitchford, *The Ultimate Book of Investment Quotations* (Capstone, Dover, NH, 1999), p. 332.

17 Table adapted from Damodaran (1996), p. 177. Other studies show that there is an excess monthly return of 1.83 per cent in the 1963 to 1990 period for stocks with low P/BV; i.e. E.F. Fama and K.R. French, 'The cross-section of expected stock returns', *Journal of Finance*, June (1992), p. 436.

18 Janet C. Lowe, *Warren Buffett Speaks: Wit and Wisdom from the World's Greatest Investor* (Wiley, New York, 1997), p. 189.

19 H. Nejat Seyhun, 'Insiders' profits, costs of trading, and market efficiency', *Journal of Financial Economics*, 16, 2 (1986), pp. 189–212. Study of period 1975–81, covering 59,148 trades, showed purchases were followed by price rises of 4.3 per cent while sales were followed by falls of –2.2 per cent.

20 In early 2001 the Association of Investment Management and Research (AIMR) established a task force to examine the issue of recommendations. Many investment banks have also issued internal guidelines to reinforce 'Chinese walls' between analysts and corporate financiers.

21 Michael C. Jensen, 'The performance of mutual funds, 1948–1967', *Journal of Finance*, 23, 2 (1968), pp. 389–416.

22 Clark Holloway, 'A note on testing an aggressive investment strategy using Value Line Ranks', *Journal of Finance*, 36, 3 (1981), pp. 711–19.

23 According to one study using past data from the NYSE, if you buy on the second to last day of the tax year and sell on the fourth day of the tax year you would have gained 6.9 per cent each and every year and more for smaller companies. You might have thought arbitrageurs would have recognized this and piled into the market before the tax year-end, then sold after it. Prices would have adjusted to remove the benefit of the anomaly.

Some say the effect has disappeared for smaller US stocks. But apparently it isn't universally the case; other studies indicate the anomaly persists. It may be that it is the arbitrageurs themselves who are doing the tax selling.

24 Kenneth French, 'Stock returns and the weekend effect', *Journal of Economics*, 8, 1 (1980), pp. 55–70. French suggests that it should be possible to benefit by always selling on a Friday and buying on a Monday or going short of the same stock on a Friday and covering your short position the following Monday. This effect may be linked to the tendency of firms to release bad news when markets are closed.

25 As did Nobel Prize winner, Myron Scholes, to the suggestion that LTCM undertake some bets on the currency markets. However, other bets were not quite as prudent.

26 Treasury's *Smaller Quotes Companies Report*, November 1998, quoted in Tony Golding, *The City: The Great Expectations Machine* (Pearson Education, London, 2001).

27 Bing Liang, 'Hedge fund performance: 1990–1999', *Financial Analysts Journal*, 57, 1 (2001), p. 11. Liang uses the TASS database which although comprehensive does not cover all global funds. According to Richard Hills there were 5000 hedge funds globally worth $300bn at the end of 1999.

2

The noise trading revolution

The stock exchanges are necessary auxiliaries of modern industry and commerce; and the services which they render to the public probably outweigh many times the evils which they cause to it. (Alfred Marshall)[1]

The line separating investment and speculation, which is never bright and clear, becomes blurred still further when most market participants have recently enjoyed triumphs. Nothing sedates rationality like large doses of effortless money. (Warren Buffett)[2]

WHAT IS NOISE TRADING?

In the bull market of the 1990s it became more apparent to me than ever before that many investors choose to react not to new facts of significance, but rather to make their trades on the basis of market rumour and noise. They follow superficial advice from ill-informed journalists or gurus and trade their portfolios more for the pleasure of seeming activity than for profit.

Investors are able to convince themselves that they are making an investment, but why should their choice of security go up? The most likely answer is that they think there is safety in numbers: everyone else is buying so they should too. But of course it is not always safe for the little fish to swim with the sharks. Such investors are relying on: (a) everyone else doing the same; (b) everyone else continuing to do the same when the price has gone up. We turn later to how bulletin boards actively facilitate the formation of this crowd psychology.

Many will sell winning stocks or hold onto sinking ones in the hope that they might recover. They will buy heavily advertised issues at the top of a boom and sell them in a bust. Some swear by technical analysis and spend their days looking at pictures of charts and indicators and nothing else. All of these are trading on noise rather than information.

> If people invest on the basis of a random guess or a hunch, a bulletin board posting, broker gossip or a groundless tip, then they are noise trading.

Let's start by distinguishing between noise and information.[3] Responding to noise is not the same as responding to information. If people invest on the basis of a random guess or a hunch, a bulletin board posting, broker gossip or a groundless tip, then they are noise trading. This is investment on the basis of what people mistakenly think is new information.

Am I a noise trader or an information trader?

A noise trader is someone who buys and sells securities on the basis of factors like commentary on bulletin boards, market gossip, newspaper tips or stale news.

An information trader acts on the release of previously non-public, brand new information that is considered material for the company's future earnings.

I should say straight up, if you haven't already guessed, that to my mind noise investing is an act of confusion. It is a kind of prejudice against or in favour of a particular stock for which every trade is a vote in favour or against. It is trading for the sake of trading, perhaps out of enjoyment. It is certainly not information. Even so it can move prices if enough people take the same view.

Following on from noise investing is *herd investing*: 'the trend is your friend'; 'running with the herd'. Whenever I hear such expressions I always run in the opposite direction. I am a natural contrarian investor. Herd investors do the opposite. They are desperate to conform at any cost. This is particularly so when those you want to mimic are making big profits. You fear you are going to be left out. Some people are by nature conformists. They learned that behaving themselves in class leads to praise from teachers. Obeying the rules in the office leads to promotion. If they see a queue they join it.

> Herd investors are desperate to conform at any cost.

The trouble is that price bubbles can develop when noise traders start chasing a trend. They begin reacting not to any particular information but solely to the fact that prices are going up. In these cases the price becomes the key information.

> There is nothing more irrational than a man who is rationally irrational. (Lecomte Du Nuoy)[4]

INTERNET BULLETIN BOARDS:
THE NOISE TRADING REVOLUTION

The internet has come into its own as a medium for sharing information about the financial markets and trading online. In the USA there are nearly 20 million internet brokerage accounts. In the UK there were 327,000 online accounts in the third quarter of 2001 and 20 per cent of trades are now done on the internet.

Information sources have proliferated. All official US company news is filed online at the EDGAR site. All UK companies file their news with the RNS service and releases are available at financial sites such as Ample Interactive Investor and Hemmington Scott. Along with these official filings there is the output of newswire journalists and stock market pundits. The internet also offers the facility for millions of investors to share their views in open bulletin boards and forums. Typically, sites such as Raging Bull and Ample Interactive Investor offer a message board for each security allowing stock specific discussion as well as 'off topic' boards for particular subjects of common interest.

Do bulletin boards affect stock prices?

Bulletin boards are often quick to post new information, leaked or official. SmithKline Beecham's merger with Glaxo and the merger between AOL and Time Warner appeared on the boards prior to the event. Oracle's stock plunged 30 per cent on false rumours spread on message boards that founder Larry Ellison had died.

Experts on a topic may choose to post their proprietary analysis on the boards. Perusing the boards can be a good indicator of popular investor sentiment, certainly as good an indicator as asking one particular stockbroker what the sentiment towards a stock is like. Other indicators of pessimism or optimism may be hidden from investors (selling stock short may, for instance, be impossible).

Boards can be vehicles for ramping a company's share price by posting falsely positive messages in order for a ramper to sell the stock at inflated levels. In February 1999 the stock price of a small Milwaukee toy company, Alottafun Inc, soared 382 per cent based on speculation in internet chat rooms. In the UK, a bulletin board poster under the name of Sixpack posted a doctored press release on the Minmet plc board, causing its price to fall. A hoaxer can deramp a stock in order to short it – sell stock he does not own in order to buy it back at lower prices. In the case of Minmet, the hoaxer posted a press release saying that the largest institutional shareholder had sold out. The Kent fraud squad are believed to be still investigating the case.

> ... Boards can be vehicles for ramping a company's share price by posting falsely positive messages in order for a ramper to sell the stock at inflated levels. ...

Early studies showed that the volume of internet messages about a stock predicted changes in the next day's stock volume and returns. In particular it was found that a doubling of overnight message volume leads to a 0.18 per cent average abnormal return.[5] Another study did not find much predictive power, but on days with high message activity there was unusually high trading volume. Changes in investor opinion correlated with abnormal returns. It was also found that boards with positive opinions are very responsive to recent positive market returns. The number of messages can be predicted by the previous day's trading volume. So the market predicts activity on the boards – not the other way around.[6]

Even if they do not affect stock prices, participants or other noise-traders may think that they do (see Figure 2.1). This may exaggerate the effect of any sentiments expressed on the boards. For me noise trading is also an act of confusion about what the stock market is for. In many countries an aversion to the stock market as a forum for rational investment develops in response to some national economic trauma. This happened, for example, in Germany after the inflation of the early twentieth century and in the USA after the Great Crash of 1929. To many it remains an iniquitous gambling house.

John Maynard Keynes is well known for his economic theories, but he was also no mean investor. As Bursar of King's College, Cambridge, Keynes was faced with constant opposition from his fellows to his apparently radical policy of selling properties and reallocating the proceeds into

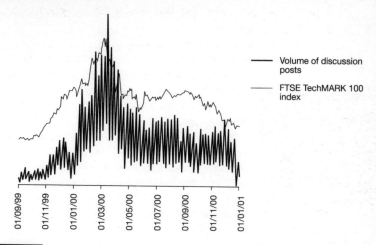

Volume of discussion posts

FTSE TechMARK 100 index

Figure 2.1 Volume of discussion postings on the Ample Interactive Investor discussion boards 1 September 1999 to 1 January 2001. There is a close match to the performance of the FTSE TechMARK 100 index of technology stocks.

the stock market. The College Estates Committee regarded stockmarket investments as mere speculation. Keynes retorted that he would rather be a 'speculator' in an asset that at least had a daily price quotation and was liquid enough to be bought and sold on a stock market than an 'investor' in something with a largely unknown price.[7] I am inclined to side with Keynes that what some would regard as speculation is in fact intelligent investment.

PROFESSIONALS VS. INDIVIDUAL INVESTORS

In the USA, as in other countries, the story of the stock market in the last 50 years has been a story of the growth of professional investors. There are now over 30 companies in the USA with assets under management of more than $100bn. Once the generation of investors haunted by the Great Crash of 1929 and the bitter depression of the early 1930s had faded away, a new crop of individual stockholders graduated. Thirty years after 1929 they numbered one in every eight adults in the USA. Against a background of immigration and a lucky escape from most of the discontinuities of World War II, the US economy has grown dramatically. Culturally the attitude to risk taking is not as conservative as in many other countries. The spoils of this growth have enriched millions of individual investors.

Although there are still many private investors, the share of the US stock market held by institutions has grown tremendously; from 26 per cent in 1980 to 53 per cent in 1996 with the increase being even greater for larger stocks. The story is much the same in the UK where 12 million people now own shares. Nearly a third of the UK population has been handed shares free from demutualized financial companies. The institutions have also grown. Whereas the private investor held 54 per cent of shares in 1963, by 1998 they held only 16.7 per cent of UK shares.[8]

WHO GETS THE INFORMATION FIRST?

The old world of cosy meetings between companies and analysts, in which prospects and information were conveyed as codes and clues, is dying. Companies are under increasing pressure to equalize the flow of information, while also being under pressure for transparency. Similarly, analysts are under pressure to be unbiased and independent. In the USA, the SEC responded to pressure from the press and investors by ruling that companies must not favour particular groups of investors by selective provision of information. Regulation FD (Fair Disclosure) has prompted a lively debate on Wall Street about whether it has forced companies to provide more timely information to the market or clam up.[9] Warren Buffett, the legendary investor, is on hand to provide an appropriate viewpoint:

> Companies are under increasing pressure to equalize the flow of information, while also being under pressure for transparency.

> Through the selectively dispersed hints, winks and nods that companies engaged in, speculatively-minded institutions and advisors were given an information edge over investment-oriented individuals. This was corrupt behaviour, unfortunately embraced by both Wall Street and corporate America. Thanks to Chairman Levitt [of the SEC], whose general efforts on behalf of

investors were both tireless and effective, corporations are now required to treat all of their owners equally.[10]

In some ways Warren Buffett is really the great professional individual investor writ large, except that he does not buy just a few shares, instead he buys the whole company.

In the UK, the authorities have been much slower to provide official rulings in favour of equitable information distribution, relying on the fact that Stock Exchange rules already require it. Unfortunately, through sloppy practice or deliberate intent, companies continue to give selective briefings to analysts and takeover information continues to be passed to journalists over the weekend (referred to in the City of London as the 'Friday night drop'). While official stock exchange news releases are now available in both countries, only in the USA are private briefings simultaneously distributed to all. It seems likely that before long new information will be available for everyone to attempt to try and decipher.

As the technology bubble collapsed, analysts came under increasing fire in the USA and UK for their apparent lack of independence from the corporate departments of the investment banks that commonly employ them. In simple terms, they were backing the house stocks. Any company that favoured the investment bank with its business could expect favourable coverage from the same house's analysts. In the USA, the analysts' professional body, AIMR, established a task force in 2001 to examine the issue. At the time of writing several investment banks were enthusiastically barring their analysts from owning any of the shares they write about.

KNOW THYSELF

Overconfidence: trading on noise, trading too often, confusion from appetite for profits

One idle summer's afternoon in London, I put together a poll on the Ample Interactive Investor website with the following question: *In respect of your driving ability are you an average, above average or below average driver?* Only 8.8 per cent of respondents said that they were below average. Of course, this cannot be true. What the poll shows is that over 90 per cent of respondents think that they are either average or above average. People are overconfident of their driving ability and also underestimate the ability of others. A poll held at the same time, which asked people what the change in their stock market investments over the last year or so showed, revealed that a third had lost over 40 per cent of their capital. I wonder if these were the same people: the average investor evidently believes that he is smarter than the average investor.[11]

Overconfidence is everywhere, particularly in money matters. If people were not overconfident, fewer would start small businesses. Proof that their confidence was misplaced is the fact that a large percentage of small businesses fail. This is a harsh tale to have to tell – you are not as smart as you think, but if it is any consolation neither am I. Overconfidence can be your downfall in a variety of ways. As investors we do not assess risky gambles in a fully rational manner. We fail properly to consider the facts in hand. We sell winners too soon and hold onto our losers for too long. We put too much weight on optimistic forecasts. Men in particular are more overconfident than women. Investors remember their past records selectively and are biased in their interpretation of their own skill.

Overconfidence on a wide scale can lead to an overreacting market with stocks going up too far in response to new information before investors come to their senses and the price falls back. Equally, if investors are confident that a conservative view of a stock is appropriate, then that stock will underreact to good news (Figure 2.2).

How can we spot if we are overconfident investors? Telltale signs are:

- chucking large amounts of cash into the market without knowing much about what we are investing in;
- thinking we have a good record and only remembering the best trades we have done in the past;
- assuming that investing in what you know is all you need for success.

And how can we learn from this discovery?

- Stop investing on every plausible sounding idea you hear.
- Do more research.
- Take professional advice.
- Like driving, you may need the occasional refresher course.

There is another area in which our appetites for certain profit can mislead us of the true odds. When given a certain gain people prefer to take the cash upfront, yet given a certain loss people will gamble. When offered a

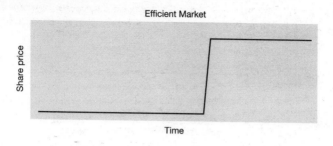

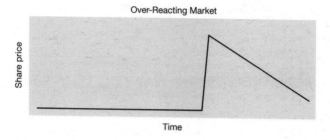

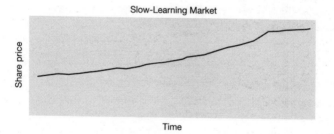

Figure 2.2 As the graphs illustrate there are three distinct types of market reaction to consider: efficient market, slow reacting market and overreacting market

Source: Asweth Damodaran, (1996) *Investments Valuation* (Chichester: Wiley), p. 168. This material is used by permission of John Wiley & Sons, Inc.

test choice between getting a five-pound note for free and a one in two chance of winning a ten-pound note, most investors will cut and run. They will take the guaranteed five pounds, proving that they are averse to risk.

In theory they should go for the ten-pound note because the probability of returns is mathematically equal. Most people don't like maths.

They didn't do well at maths at school and they never want to have to learn dull algebra ever again. Hence they can't even do a simple probability calculation. When the tables are turned and you have a choice of giving someone else a five-pound note or a one in two chance of winning a ten-pound note most investors will gamble on the ten-pound bet. In this case they prefer to take on the risk.

> The moral is to let winners run and cut losses.

In the markets, if you have a losing share you prefer to take on the risk that it may go down more by hanging onto it for dear life in the hope that things will turn out all right. Equally, when a stock you own has gone up, you prefer to bank the winner and lose out on the fact that the stock may go up some more. The moral is to let winners run and cut losses.

FRAMES – IT'S THE WAY YOU TELL 'EM

Take two politicians with different views talking about the same thing, for example, the legalization of cannabis. One side presents the good points about it – less street crime; the other presents the bad points – encouraging addiction. If only one of the two was present you would probably walk away thinking that one point of view was very reasonable. Your view would be anchored in the frame of their argument. So it is with investing. If you just get half the story, you end up taking the wrong decision.

First impressions last. For instance, a group of surveyors was given a pack of information and told that the recent asking price of a property was $120,000 dollars. They valued it on average at $114,000. A different group was given the same information but told that the asking price was $150,000. They produced a value of $129,000.[12] When we are anchoring our decision we latch onto some fact and can't get it out of our heads. For example, we may have seen Vodafone at £5 per share. When we see it next at £1.50 the price doesn't seem right.

How can you tell whether you are suffering from anchoring ailments?

- Do you make decisions on the hoof without a moment's thought?
- Do you always buy your favourite brands?
- Are you unable to sell investments for less than you paid for them?

If this is you, then you are a chronic victim of anchoring.

What is this doctor's prescription for anchoring?

- Get a second opinion.
- Do your research.
- Don't pay more attention to the share price than the fundamentals.
- Forget the past, it is the future that counts.

THE WAY WE FIND THINGS OUT

Heuristic rules of thumb for investing

If we glance at something and it looks familiar, we instantly label it as something we already know: if it walks like a duck and looks like a duck, it probably is a duck. But we may be wrong. We may be missing some important detail. When you learn a foreign language it is often the case that you cannot find a word for something you want to describe. French, for instance, has several different categories for the word friend. So when French people are looking for an English word to describe some delicate level of intimacy, they cannot find it.

Words and concepts such as illiquid, GNP, Retail Price Index or 'beating the index', which are in common use today, were totally unknown in popular speech 50 or 60 years ago. Words are powerful ways of defining and summarizing things and getting them under control in our minds, but in so doing we may miss the point. We may define whole categories of company as 'quality' stocks, 'bios' or 'techs'. Dot com, an expression which once had a very positive connotation, now has the opposite. We may well be wrong. If one type of stock is so good, everybody who agrees may already have bought their fill. If a stock is so bad, those who share that view may have sold out. Investors who swallow such rules of thumb become overly pessimistic about past losses and over-optimistic about past winners.

Behavioural finance is a very ambitious area. It is looking to answer the most difficult questions you can think of. For example: How do investors view and evaluate risk? Why do they gamble? It may surprise you to learn that around 1.1 per cent of US men are compulsive gamblers.[13] Other puzzles include how bubbles get going and why investors trade so much. If you could work out the answers to these questions you would be halfway to getting very rich indeed.

THE INFORMATION WHEEL CAN TURN

Short-circuiting the wheel

Professional investors have traditionally been passive investors. In my years in fund management there was a daily ritual of meetings with the chief executives and finance directors of large companies who once a year would devote a fortnight or so to doing the City rounds of investment institutions. They would arrive at the offices, spend an hour or so giving an update on the company and its markets, answer a few mostly ill-informed questions and then leave, not to return until the following year. They would usually tell us how it was, giving us the bad news straight and making the odd promise. If we didn't like what we heard we often sold, knowing that no one institution, even if we owned a couple of per cent, was really powerful enough to make much difference. What we were looking for was reliable and predictable growth. As Tony Golding, a City fund manager, points out: 'Investors abhor uncertainty. They have a deep-rooted desire to make world a more predictable place.'[14]

But increasingly, when things go wrong investment institutions have begun to get active. When British Airways failed to deliver, the Chief Executive, Robert Ayling, had to go. The same thing happened in the summer of 2001 at Marconi after a bungled profits warning. Institutions have been willing to step in with a demand for change in the interests of shareholders. In Golding's words: 'In 1990 when recession hit, institutions found themselves forced to adopt a more interventionist stance towards their investments.'[15] This trend has accelerated as more active foreign investors have acquired more shares. In 1963 foreigners owned 7 per cent of UK shares; at the end of 1998 they owned 27.6 per cent.

> Investors abhor uncertainty. They have a deep-rooted desire to make world a more predictable place.

George Soros, the legendary speculator who shorted $10bn of the pound sterling and broke the Bank of England's attempt to defend a high value of sterling in 1992, takes this argument further. In his view investing is a reflexive process. The activity of investors can influence the company, just as the activity of the company can influence the investors and share price.

The connection between the stock prices and the underlying companies is not a one-way traffic. Stock market valuations first have an immediate impact on things such as the motivational value to employees of share options. A depressed share price can undermine confidence in a company's ability to repay its debt and make that debt more expensive to obtain. If a company wishes to issue shares, then a high share price can make it easy to do so and a low share price can make it expensive and difficult. In his biography Soros says: 'I do not accept the proposition that stock prices are a passive reflection of underlying values, nor do I accept the proposition that the reflection tends to correspond to the underlying value. I contend that values are always distorted.'[16]

Soros clearly sees that the views of participants are part of the situation in which they are both observers and possessors of a voting power. They can revalue the shares up or down by their own trading activity. When this happens the information wheel can begin to turn (Figure 2.3). Instead of information cascading down from the company at the top to the investors at the bottom, the flow is reversed. The investors are in control at the top and the company is haplessly sinking to the bottom. In such cases the price has become the key item of information.

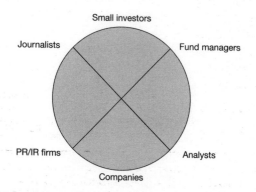

Figure 2.3   The information wheel begins to turn

THE INDIVIDUAL INVESTOR ADVANTAGE

Markets have a way of seeking out weakness. In the eternal competition between bulls and bears, one or the other party gives greater credence to particular items of information. They interpret the information differently. Bulletin boards are one of the subtle ways in which the different parties expose the extent of their pessimism or optimism. When there is no news, and no news really can be good news, there are always new bulletin boards to read or gossip to pass on.

Individual investors, armed with the power of their personal computers, are using a level of complexity that was not available even to professional fund managers five or ten years ago. They are also furnished with a

> Markets have a way of seeking out weakness.

means of two-way communication. They can interrogate remote and formerly inaccessible databases. They can post proxy votes electronically. Most importantly private investors can now receive official news releases at the same time as the institutional investors and analysts. They can, at least potentially, short circuit the information wheel, removing the information advantage cherished by professional investors.

Individual investors can create market noise, but they also have access to the tools to tune it out. Once again here is the plan of the book:

- Understand your own investing behaviour. Know the great bubbles. Understand overconfidence, overtrading and misleading frameworks.

- Understand the investing behaviour of the professionals. Learn from the master investors.

- Jump on the information wheel. Know when you have spotted really new information.

- Know the market anomalies – growth stocks, small firms effect, ratios effects and calendar effects.

- Build a winning, balanced portfolio using professional tools – broker research, online information, screens and online portfolios.

NOTES

1 Alfred Marshall, *Money, Credit and Commerce* (Macmillan, London, 1923), p. 95.

2 Chairman's Letter to the Shareholders, 2001.

3 Peter Bernstein, *Capital Ideas* (Free Press, New York, 1993), p. 124.

4 Dean LeBaron and Romesh Vaitlingham with Marilyn Pitchford, *The Ultimate Book of Investment Quotations* (Capstone, Dover, NH, 1999), p. 224.

5 P. Wysocki, 'Cheap talk on the web: the determinants of postings on stock message boards'. (Working paper, University of Michigan Business School, 1999).

6 R. Tumarkin, and Whitelaw, R.F. 'News or noise? Internet postings and stock prices', *Financial Analysts Journal*, May/June (2001), pp. 41–51.

7 *The Collected Writings of John Maynard Keynes*, Donald Moggridge (ed), Vol. XII. (Cambridge University Press, New York, 1983), p. 109. With permission of Palgrave.

8 Office for National Statistics, *Share Ownership, A Report on the Ownership of Shares as at 31st December 1998* (The Stationery Office, London, 1999), p. 7.

9 A number of surveys have been conducted to cast light on this debate. The evidence does not produce an unambiguous verdict. A National Investor Relations Institute's survey of 600 companies, published in February, shows an increase of information being disclosed to the public as a result of regulation FD. Another NIRI survey found that 48 per cent of companies were releasing the same amount of information as they were before, while 24 per cent were releasing less and 28 per cent more. And, according to First Call/Thomson Financial, regulation FD seems to be leading more companies to issue press releases when they want to update investors on earnings prospects. But a Securities Institute Association survey was, by contrast, less positive, suggesting a net loss of disclosure. (Howard Davies, Chairman of the FSA, Speech to the Investor Relations Society, 9 July 2001)

10 Warren Buffett in Chairman's Letter to the Shareholders of Berkshire Hathaway Inc., 2000.

11 Adam Smith, in his famous treatise *Wealth of Nations* (1776), said: 'The overwhelming conceit which the greater part of men have of their abilities is an ancient evil remarked by the philosophers and moralists of all ages.'

12 John B. Taylor and Michael Woodford (eds), *Handbook of Macroeconomics*, Vol. 1 (North-Holland, Amsterdam, 1999), pp. 1305–40. There is another good (and short) summary of behavioural finance: Alistair Byrne, 'A study of how investors make stupid mistakes', *Professional Investor*, Dec/Jan (2000–1), p. 13.

13 John B. Taylor and Michael Woodford (eds), *Handbook of Macroeconomics*, Vol. 1, (North-Holland, Amsterdam, 1999), pp. 1305–40.

14 Tony Golding, *The City: Inside the Great Expectations Machine* (Pearson Education, London, 2001), p. 60.

15 Tony Golding, *The City: Inside the Great Expectations Machine* (Pearson Education, London, 2001), p. 171.

16 George Soros, *The Alchemy of Finance* (Simon and Schuster, New York, 1987), p. 48.

3

Fundamental analysis

Part One: Picking a good stock

A qualitative decision

How can we detect a company's growth?

Yikes, numbers: ratio analysis

Hidden assets

Selecting stocks using P/E models

Shells and penny shares

Picking a good management

Big ideas: behavioural finance and mean reversion

Market timing

Part Two: Picking a good industry

Looking at different industries

Detecting earnings quality

Corporate events: mergers, takeovers and IPOs

In the old days any well-trained security analyst could do a professional job of selecting undervalued issues through detailed studies; but in light of the enormous amount of research being carried out, I doubt whether, in most cases, such extensive efforts will generate sufficiently superior selections to justify the cost. (Benjamin Graham)[1]

The real accomplishment of the many thousand analysts now studying not so many thousand companies is the establishment of proper relative prices in today's market for most of the leading issues and a great many secondary ones. (Benjamin Graham and David L. Dodd)[2]

Part One: Picking a good stock

A QUALITATIVE DECISION

When you come to select a stock for your portfolio there may seem to be an overwhelming volume of detail about the various companies and their industries. All of it may seem important. But it is a measure of your skill as an investor that you learn to discriminate. While it is useful to have

> In the end you are going to have to make a qualitative decision.

lots of tables of numbers or lists of statistics, quantitative information can be superficially definitive. Numbers can get out of date very quickly. Managers of companies can manipulate accounting data by choosing one practice or another.

In the end you are going to have to make a qualitative decision. It is a good idea to look at the relevant quantitative information, but that alone is not enough. Of course this may make you feel uncomfortable. We all prefer to deal in black and white. But in making an investment we are taking on a risk and while our risk should be compensated with a good return there are no money-back guarantees.

HOW CAN WE DETECT A COMPANY'S GROWTH?

Many investors start by looking at the share price and its graph first, as though that conveyed all the information they needed to know. To my mind the price is merely the effect of a variety of root causes – the smoke above the fire. My own starting point is to find the basic facts, most often in the annual report. If I have a hunch that there are good growth prospects in a particular industry or subsector, I put together the reports of a group of companies for comparison. In each report I start with the chairman's statement to get a flavour of the company's products and current market conditions. I then turn to the cash flows and accounts to try and get some idea of the scale of the company. Last I check things like share price, yield, dividend cover, P/E ratios and Price/Book ratios. These help refine whether there is value in the share at the current price.

Growth is the holy grail of stock market investment. Without growth, earnings and dividends cannot grow. Not just the fact of growth but also the direction of change in growth needs to be examined. Is it increasing or is it slowing down? We are less interested in the past than in the future and we are just as interested that a company can afford to fund its growth as we are in a company producing growth for growth's sake. Companies can quite literally grow broke if they are not careful. The individuals tasked with forecasting earnings growth are for the most part stockbroking analysts, which is quite a job as we shall see.

> Growth is the holy grail of stock market investment.

It is worthwhile stating the obvious fact that most growth comes from increasing sales of products. So it is often useful to look at the companies' key products and preferably a graph of their sales. As shown in Figure 3.1, we can see weekly sales of new products, such as DVDs or a new computer chip, over a number of weeks. At first the growth is very fast, but eventually it hits a peak and falls to a stable level. The accumulated sales are also visible. It should be evident that the growth curve is fairly predictable for all products of any kind.

Once an analyst establishes the target maximum penetration for a product, he or she can then work out the growth rate taking into account the useful life of the device and the replacement rate. The obvious reality check is the number of households in the country. For big ticket consumer

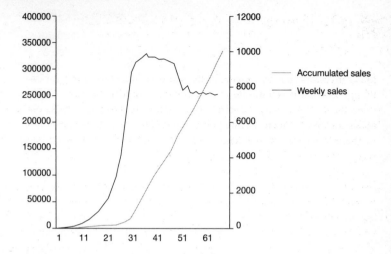

Figure 3.1 Weekly sales of a new product (right-hand scale) and the accumulated sales of that product over time (left-hand scale). Growth rates are initially very fast but slow to a more stable level

Source: Fred Wellings (1998), 'Profits forecasting: a practitioner's view', *Professional Investor*, October, p. 28.

durables such as widescreen TVs and bagless vacuum cleaners, you are unlikely to have much more than one item per household at any one time.

Forecasting profits is not quite the same as making a sales forecast because between revenues and profits there are expenses, interest, taxes and all manner of accounting. Over the years, analysts and industry watchers will develop a mental filing cabinet of pictures of all the trends and cycles in their industries.[3] There is a familiar pattern of a company having a J-shaped curve of product sales when the new product is introduced which then falls off as the potential ownership or market is satisfied. Repetitive patterns are not just for the chartists.

Once the industry growth rates are discovered, sales forecasting is a matter of working out market share, which is usually a function of the marketing expenditure. If you can spot that rising, then market share will usually follow. Analysts go on to calculate margins and profitability and then construct elaborate accounts using historic figures as the basis and cash flowing through from sales into the accounts.

At a product level, the success or failure of the product being sold will usually depend on whether there is differentiation or a cost advantage in the product. It may be that the company has a technology advantage or innovative designs. An example of this would be Cartier, the Swiss jewels and watches company. In this case the main threats are going to be imitation or a change in technology.

If the firm has set out to be the low-cost producer in its industry, its success will depend on large scale and minimizing costs. An example would be Ford, the motor company. Threats to a company like Ford would be a competitor finding a cheaper manufacturing process or a drastic change in customer taste.

Where a company is growing too fast it will need to raise capital by issuing more stock or getting new bank credit. If it is growing too slowly it can give up the ghost and return money to shareholders or acquire growth through acquisition. Growth can be as much of a burden as a badge of success. 'It is a sad fact that almost as many companies can go bankrupt because they grew too fast as do those that grew too slowly.'[4]

> **Where can I check analyst forecasts?** Individual analyst forecasts and copies of their research are now widely available on the internet. You can consult the Reuters or Extel survey to find out the most popular analysts, and then check out their latest forecasts on websites such as Ample Interactive Investor and Hemmington Scott. Finally you can download their research using the websites listed in the final part of this book.

YIKES, NUMBERS: RATIO ANALYSIS

It is inevitable, even for those of us who are not mathematically inclined, that the investment process will involve taking at least a brief glance at one or two numerals. Companies report their performance over a particular period in the form of accounts. These can be easily analyzed in order to detect trends and compare with other like companies or industries. We can then build these trends and comparisons into our forecasts.

Ratios are not just for analysts. They are easy to calculate and can serve as useful comparative tools. If you are stuck on which of two similar shares to invest in, calculate a couple of ratios and go for the one that comes out best. Think of ratios as only part of the picture. You cannot expect simply dividing one number by another to give the whole story of a complex organization, but it may help you on your way to understanding the company better (Table 3.1).

> Ratios are not just for analysts. They are easy to calculate and can serve as useful comparative tools.

Table 3.1 Using different ratios – objectives, pros and cons

Type of ratio	Objective of consulting ratio	Pros	Cons
P/E	Low P/Es show you can buy the earnings cheap.	Easy to compare. Can work out with next year's earnings forecast.	Management can flatter earnings. Different industries not comparable.
Operating margin	High margin = high profitability.	Easy to compare like companies.	'Aggressive accounting'.
Price/Book	Low Price/Book shows you can buy the assets cheap.	More stable than P/E and easy to make comparisons.	Assets in the books at old values.
Gearing	High gearing = higher risk.	Useful for similar companies.	Some debt can be hidden.
Asset turnover	High asset turnover = good use of assets.	Useful for asset-intensive industries.	Some industries don't need lots of assets.
Return on equity (ROE)	High ROE = good return on its equity.	Easy to compare.	Value of the equity gets outdated.

P/E and Price/Book are very commonly discussed in the financial press. Price divided by earnings, the P/E ratio, is a useful comparative tool. It is also very sensitive to changes in earnings, say if a company is restructuring or experiencing a downturn. There is no right or wrong P/E.

Profitability is easily calculated by working out the operating margin. Operating income (sometimes called profit before interest and tax) is divided by sales. Both the inputs into this ratio are easily found on the profit and loss account (P&L). Sales are the top line and operating income is below cost of goods sold. Take care that you are using the correct year's figure. As with earnings, this ratio can be sensitive to 'aggressive accounting'; for example, if the management does not have a conservative policy on booking in sales from its longer run contracts.

Price as a multiple of book value is a more stable measure, but again there is no right or wrong P/B ratio. A lot depends on the management's policy of valuing their book assets and lots of companies don't need lots of assets. Compare the assets of a chemical company with those of a provider of consulting services.

Leverage or gearing is also easily worked out from the balance sheet. You just find the entry for long-term debt in the bottom half of the balance sheet and divide it into the total assets line found in the middle.

Asset turnover is another easy number to find. You simply divide the sales figure from the profit and loss by the total assets number found in the middle of the balance sheet.

The final ratio I intend to inflict on you is Return on Equity (ROE). This is very simply the net income divided by the shareholders' equity. Net income is on the P&L while shareholders' equity is on the balance sheet near the bottom.

These ratios are especially useful when comparing between years so that the trend is revealed. There is no one correct ratio. A judgement that a ratio is too high just depends on your point of view. For instance, a company may have high leverage because it has geared up to invest in a good project. A company may have low asset turnover because that is a typical feature of a capital-intensive industry. Margins may be low because the company is experiencing a cyclical downturn and has high fixed costs.

Each ratio is particularly sensitive to both of the inputs into the equation. For instance, the intellectual property (patents on drugs and drugs in development) of pharmaceutical companies is not included as part of their equity. Although they benefit from the employment of intellectual assets, they are not on the balance sheet. So the return on equity for pharmaceutical companies is artificially higher than for other industries.

Similarly the accounting choices made by management on the presentation of earnings can sharply affect the inputs of the ratios. If earnings are flattered by one device or another, then so are the ratios. There are big differences internationally: for example, US and UK companies tend to be financed by the sale of shares, whereas French and German companies tend to issue debt. This affects leverage ratios. However, comparing one company's ratio to another within its industry provides a useful shortcut to ranking a company among its fellows.

HIDDEN ASSETS

Many private investors seem to be spellbound by assets and treat them as an investment screen, sniffing out companies with the most assets and the lowest Price/Book ratio. A lot of the blame for this falls on Benjamin Graham, one of the earliest investment theorists. He was rooted in the dark days of the US Depression when bankruptcy lurked around every corner. In his investing, Graham's insurance policy was the question: 'Is this company worth more dead or alive?' In the inflationary late twentieth century this investing approach had a revival, but now even private investors are deploying a more sophisticated approach.

> In his investing, Graham's insurance policy was the question: 'Is this company worth more dead or alive?'

There are hidden assets, but of course they have to be balanced against hidden liabilities. The main hidden jewels are intangible assets such as patents, brand names, copyrights, licences and leasehold assets, as well as research and development (R&D) in progress. Details of these are not usually in the accounts, although they can be guessed at from the price obtained when they change hands.

Other hidden assets often sought out by investors are property and real estate companies and investment trusts. These may trade below their asset value for long periods, so do not expect an instant uplift. Part of this discount to assets could reflect higher risk from large borrowings or exposure to volatile assets.

SELECTING STOCKS USING P/E MODELS

Choosing stocks can seem like hard work. We are all on the lookout for an easy shortcut and investment screens can do a lot of the hard work for you. The most common screens all use P/E ratios. Computers add up the P/E ratio of all stocks in the market and sort them out with the lowest P/E stocks at the bottom and the highest at the top.

> Choosing stocks can seem like hard work.

They also weight them all added together to arrive at a market average P/E which is called 100. Individual stocks can then be compared relative to the market average. For instance, a stock may have a P/E 20 per cent higher than the average. If the average is 10 its P/E will be 12 and its P/E relative (sometimes called PER) will be 120.

One further elaboration of this computer-driven process is the P/E growth ratio (PEG), which just divides the P/E by the earnings growth rate (next year's forecast compared to this year's historic earnings). For example, the PEG is 2 for a company with a P/E of 16 and a growth rate of 8 per cent, 16/8 = 2. All stocks are then ranked and those where you get more growth for less P/E are chosen. Some investors such as Jim Slater swear by them: 'To me, a low P/E ratio and a high growth rate has always been the right combination.'[5] They buy when PEGs are below one and sell if they head up towards two.

> **What is a PEG ratio?** A PEG ratio is the P/E divided by the firm's growth rate (for example, the PEG is 2 for a company with a P/E of 16 and a growth rate of 8 per cent, 16/8 = 2).

The trouble with all the P/E models is that they are using numbers that are often very changeable. Managers can bolster earnings by asset sales or acquisitions while stockbrokers' growth forecasts are constantly changing. Prices of stocks can also be volatile and subject to artificial swings. It is compounding flexible figures one on top of the other. The P/E itself is vulnerable to accounting manipulations – so too is the growth rate. What if the company has just bought a fast-growing company or has sacrificed current growth for investment to develop a sure-fire product? Who knows what the growth rate is going to be next year. Brokers' forecasts are notoriously inaccurate. P/E itself is already a function of growth rates, past and future. The other big input error is the market price that obviously already reflects investors' expectations about growth. So you could be building in several layers of inaccuracy.[6]

SHELLS AND PENNY SHARES

Many investors become mesmerized by stocks with a low value, as though that in itself is a guarantee that the stock will inevitably go up. It is a fact that many of the best performing stocks were those that once no respectable fund manager would want to touch. Before they got better they had to get worse. When the share price hit rock bottom, a heavyweight management team appeared and turned the company around, probably by injecting a new business.

It is quite true that some shell companies are created out of redundant floats of dead companies and these are used by entrepreneurs to obtain a listed vehicle and create a company. But with so many such shells about it would seem an aimless

> Many investors become mesmerized by stocks with a low value, as though that in itself is a guarantee that the stock will inevitably go up.

task to be guessing which one the entrepreneurs are going to target next.

PICKING A GOOD MANAGEMENT

Picking a good company is to a great extent a question of avoiding a bad management. There is no point having the best factories, highly qualified employees and stacks of cash in the bank if the men at the top of the company throw it all away on living the good life or doing a dud deal. Indeed, the story of many large companies has been one of tug-of-war between shareholders and bad managements.

When shareholders have the upper hand, companies are run for their benefit. When incumbent management think they can pay little attention to shareholders, then increasing the share price is not a priority. From the 1980s onwards many hostile takeovers were launched with the precise objective of forcing bad managements to restructure their companies. Investors can often spot bad managements by the kind of industry in which they operate. Prime candidates are often found in mature or declining industries. With few profitable investment opportunities, managers might

> More frivolous but obvious signs of bad management are corporate excesses.

be expected to shrink or withdraw from the business, perhaps returning surplus funds to shareholders. But often they do not. They continue to invest in the old way. Out of loyalty to company culture or employees and in order to retain their office and prestige, they throw money at unprofitable investments. The board of directors should in theory put matters right, but is often surprisingly ineffectual.

More frivolous but obvious signs of bad management are corporate excesses. Management may award themselves extravagant share options or salary packages with low performance targets. There may be a company jet or a fleet of limousines. The institutional investors, who own the bulk of a company's shares, would normally be expected to act as a check on this but many do not consider it their responsibility.

Good managements are wide awake to change. They are not steeped in a stuffy and self-regarding company culture closed to outside influences. They are intuitive strategists, but sensitive to the detail. They have made themselves aware of what is going on in their companies. They know what the next product is and what the customers want. Managers should know all the weaknesses and vulnerabilities of their companies and have answers ready if asked how they aim to circumvent them.

In an established company there may be a bureaucratic system of management, but they must know how to work it to ensure change can happen. For a growth company it is always a good sign if managers have a large personal stake in its success or failure. If managers are the founders and lack formal experience, then it is a positive signal if they surround themselves with well-qualified and experienced lieutenants. Personally, good managers should have the charisma to lead without the arrogance of high office. They must have credibility before the analysts, investors and backers and should not shirk tough questions in meetings with them.

How do I check out the management? You should be able to get a flavour of management from the annual reports, biographies and unedited interviews in the media or from providers such as Wall Street Transcript. The best opportunity for many private investors to meet them in person is at the annual general meetings. Just ring up the company secretary to ask the date of the next one.

BIG IDEAS: BEHAVIOURAL FINANCE AND MEAN REVERSION

Every decade has its big ideas. Behavioural finance is an attempt to explain why investors make investment decisions in a different way to how theorists think they should. We shall be looking at the ideas of behavioural finance and the efficient markets theory in more detail through the book. It is sufficient to say here that investors are complicated animals; they are human and make mistakes like everybody else. They do not behave like a scientific model and may or may not learn from their experience. The way we react to a situation today may or may not be the way we react to it tomorrow.

The other big idea floating around at the moment is mean reversion. This comes from the notion that variable things in nature such as population growth or volcanoes always settle down to some average (mean). In stock prices this implies that a high value is more likely to be followed by a lower value and vice versa. Mean reversion represents the evolution of uncertainties. For as the uncertainty continues through time it fluctuates around a constant level.[7]

> Mean reversion represents the evolution of uncertainties.

This can be applied to stock prices, commodity prices and fixed costs. In a portfolio context it means an investor thinks that whatever a security's value has been in the past, it will eventually revert to that mean value. When presented with competing investment choices, an investor will choose the one farthest below its average value. But mean reversion hasn't won over everyone. George Soros argues 'that there is little empirical evidence of an equilibrium or even a tendency for prices to move towards an equilibrium'.[8] He thinks prices are basically random.

MARKET TIMING

Many investors attribute more importance to market timing than the quality of what they are buying. The most obvious solution to the problem of timing is that it depends on the time period you are looking at. The issue is really wrapped up in the age-old distinction between speculation and investment.[9] Speculation is trading on the basis of little more than a hunch. A speculation is unlikely to be based on any significant deduction. It is motivated by a desire to get exposure to events in the future.

> Many investors attribute more importance to market timing than the quality of what they are buying.

Investment on the other hand has a more certain basis in facts. It is likely to be grounded in the question of what the stock is really worth. Investment is primarily concerned with the underlying earnings growth over time. If you are confident of the underlying value of the company you are buying, you should be prepared to pay up today for growth in future years. Speculation is more likely to be preoccupied with the price tomorrow.

You should be able to tell whether you are a speculator or an investor by the simple test of your reaction to a temporary dip in a share price. This will cause a speculator alarm but leave an investor unconcerned.

Am I a speculator or an investor?

- How long do you hold stocks for?
  (a) more than a year
  (b) I close out all my positions by 4:30 every day
- How many times do you trade a year?
  (a) less than fifteen
  (b) as often as I can, bathroom breaks permitting
- How many times have you been married?
  (a) < 2x
  (b) >2x
- How many children do you have?
  (a) 2.4
  (b) I admit to 5
- How much do you invest on each trade?
  (a) < 10 per cent of my total wealth
  (b) as much as I can borrow

If you scored mostly (a) then you are an investor; if (b) then you are a speculator!

Part Two: Picking a good industry

Almost as important as choosing the right company within an industry is identifying which industries are going to prosper and which are in terminal decline. Even the best canal builder was a poor investment when the railways came along. If an industry contains just too many competitors, profits will tumble. If it costs too little to enter an industry, say, you can just hang up a sign, then competition is likely to worsen. There may be a problem with the supply of raw materials or specialized skills. New technologies may be copying the key product at low cost. An industry might be unduly exposed to the cost of borrowing, such as leasing, or to the price of oil, such as airlines.

On the other side of the coin you should be able to identify which industries are on the up. New technologies such as the internet have lowered the cost base of industries with high mass distribution costs so you should expect the margins to rise of industries benefiting such as insurance and book sales. Some industries have exploited growing international demand for brand names, for example, soft drinks and footwear. Population data show that there is a surge of people born after the war who are now entering retirement age, so you can expect demand for healthcare and retirement homes to boom. We are looking for such big picture trends and seeking potential as yet unfulfilled. So we might have looked at mobile telephones and pagers in the late 1980s and foreseen the potential for them to be used not just by business people, as was then the case, but by ordinary consumers.

> ...... We are looking for such big picture trends and seeking potential as yet unfulfilled. ....

It is a useful exercise to classify industries into categories such as Pioneer, Growth, Maturity and Decline.[10]

1. *Pioneer*: This is the high-risk stage when product acceptance is questionable.
2. *Growth*: Product is accepted and rollout to the market begins. Execution of strategy is the main risk.
3. *Maturity*: The industry is stable and trends up and down with the general economy. Participants compete for market share.
4. *Decline*: The game is up! Shifting tastes or technologies have overtaken the industry and it goes into decline.

Evidently the riskiest stage is the Pioneer stage when companies are using up cash to develop the product and get it into the marketplace. There is a high failure rate. Seven out of ten start-ups fail to survive in the USA and nine out of ten in the UK. In a speculative bubble, start-ups will multiply to feed the demand by investors for risky assets. Many small companies more usually at home in a venture capitalist's portfolio will cash in by floating on the stock market. This was an unfortunate characteristic of the internet securities bubble of 1998 to 2000.

With the Growth stage, the big questions are how far will it grow and how fast. The best growth story is one where you recognize it early and get in at the beginning. Another sure-fire winner is where the industry has created demand that did not previously exist. Twenty years ago, who would have thought they needed a mobile phone, an e-mail account or a text-messaging viewer to stay in touch.

As competition increases, attracted by profitability, you will get maturity and after that decline. The only thing left is to battle for market share and to minimize costs. Among these last two categories you will tend to find the high dividend paying stocks and contrarian plays.

How do I find out which are the growth industries? Use our guide together with some of the online sources for different industries mentioned at the end of this book. Above all keep your ears open. If you get interested in the industry, find out the key statistic or indicator and follow the bellwether firm within that industry.

LOOKING AT DIFFERENT INDUSTRIES

Every industry has its own peculiar characteristics and key indicators. The brief guide below covers some of the main industries. If you get interested in one of the industries, your next step is to find out which is the bellwether company in that industry and what the competition is like.

Media

Media companies create and distribute intellectual property. There are three types of property produced by the media:

- information
- education
- entertainment.

The mark of a successful media company is always its ability to sell creative ideas many times over. There is a tendency for some distributors to become dependent on big name talents that can exercise control. So spotting successful media companies is about finding brands where the 'gatekeeper is king'.[11] One odd characteristic about media companies is the high concentration of ownership and the enthusiasm with which wealthy men on the make seek to acquire them as publicity machines.

Industrials

These mature and stable basic industries with lots of assets are prime candidates for ratio analysis and the use of P/E and Price/Book. Check out the broker reports for Discounted Cash Flow (DCF) analysis. While DCF has its drawbacks – it is sensitive to the discount rate chosen and to the accounting policies of management – it is a widespread method. Firms in the same subsector can be reliably compared.

What is DCF? Stable cash flow in the future can be predictably discounted back using a Discounted Cash Flow (DCF) technique to arrive at a theoretical present value today of future cash flows.

Utilities

As with industrials, these tend to be stable and mature businesses and are eminently suitable for P/E, Price/Book and DCF analysis. The main difference is that for all utilities you have to check out the regulatory situation, which has a high incidence in natural monopolies such as electricity or water supply; it is not so much the fact of regulation as the direction of regulatory change, whether it is getting more or less strict.

Banks and financials

The unique factor with these stocks is the exposure to the interest rate cycle of firms borrowing more during economic good times and then regretting it when bad times come along. Income for banks is mainly interest income, while insurance concerns will be exposed to the cycle of insurance claims and the performance of their portfolios of assets versus the attendant liabilities. Valuations on P/E and DCF can be tempered with comparison of the bad debt levels within the sector.

Oils

The chief factor to watch here is of course the price and demand for oil. Another major influence is the control and ownership of reserves, the majority of which are owned by states. An oil company must successfully replace its reserves to survive. With diversified oil companies there may be exposure to chemicals and the growth of gas. Asset value may be important, particularly if profits are not yet being generated. One problem is that the valuation of reserves can be very subjective (what is referred to in accounting as the LIFO vs. FIFO debate) and so working out the cost and size of capital can pose difficulties.[12]

Pharmaceuticals

Pharmaceutical companies are greatly dependent on the merits of very few drugs. Most drugs actually fail to reach the market and each successful drug will cost more than $100m to develop. Pharmaceuticals is a research-based industry so it is important to know how much is going into what and how it is accounted for. Since R&D is not usually a balance sheet asset, the return on capital of the industry is often overstated.

Investors need to evaluate the scientific information in the three stages of clinical trials. Phase (i) trials are the basis of whether to proceed to human testing of products. Phase (ii) trials are the first major trials of a drug to demonstrate statistical efficacy. Phase (iii) trials are designed to demonstrate conclusively the effectiveness of a drug and provide regulatory data for government approval: 'Valuation of prospects for a few major products, both those currently on the market and new drugs in R&D account for most of a pharmaceutical company's stock market value.'[13]

Property

Earnings from the rent roll of property companies may be less important to investors than the performance of the capital values of the portfolio. Quality of management can have a very direct impact on portfolios, which are often highly concentrated and illiquid. Valuation may be subjective and dependent on infrequent appraisals. Risks revolve around the cost of debt and amount of leverage. Many sectors such as breweries, transport and retail are property companies in disguise, so if you are positive on property it is worth looking at these as well.

High tech

With immature streams of earnings, high technology stocks defy conventional valuation. The most popular substitute has been to value them as a multiple of their sales, a price to sales ratio that can then be compared to like companies. But this fails to account for very different types of businesses. A second approach is the DCF approach, discounting future cash flows by a selected interest (discount) rate to come up with a present value. This suffers from the problem of sensitivity to the selected interest rate and sensitivity to the growth rates selected for the cash flows. A final group of valuations involves sophisticated probability modelling and anecdotally these have been more successful, although difficult for laymen to understand.

Mining

Assessing mining stocks is a matter of forecasting the prices of the relevant minerals. It is also a function of the quality of the reserves and the rate at which these deplete. If a company is unsuccessful in replacing reserves at reasonable cost, the long-run future of the company is in doubt. The analysis of mining stocks as a group is often a matter of valuing them all on the same basis and seeing which is cheap.[14]

DETECTING EARNINGS QUALITY

One penny of earnings from a company may not be the same thing as one penny of earnings from another company. When managers compile accounts they make important choices as to how their accounts are compiled. Three classic examples of accounting fiddles show how large a problem this can be:

> One penny of earnings from a company may not be the same thing as one penny of earnings from another company.

1. Companies in most countries can keep certain leases off their balance sheet and thus understate their real level of debt.
2. When companies restructure they can often take an excessively pessimistic write-off charge all at once so future earnings will be flattered by the use of assets that disappeared from the balance sheet in the restructuring.
3. Companies can acquire fast-growing companies and by consolidating the accounting records they can flatter their own records.

On an international level there are distinct differences in accounting rules, which make for very different looking accounts. Some countries write off the goodwill in acquisition (the difference between the purchase price and the assets purchased) immediately against reserves. Others such as the

USA charge it to income over 40 years. Germany charges it over a more punishing 15 years, while the UK uses 20 years or the useful life of the asset.

This kind of difference helps explain why, when in 1993 Daimler-Benz applied for a US listing, it had to publish two sets of accounts. The one under German rules showed a solid profit of DM600m but the one under US rules showed a staggering loss of DM1.7bn. In Japan the habit of investing excess capital into the shares of suppliers and customers has led to some very strange looking balance sheets by western standards.

A further issue is the problem of aggressive accounting practices, both here and in the USA, indeed perhaps more so in the USA. I am talking of circumstances where the financial performance of a company is presented in an unrealistically favourable light in an attempt to meet market expectation, reduce tax liabilities, comply with loan covenants or meet legal or regulatory thresholds. All of these can lead to the market being misled about a company's profitability or performance.

What are the danger signals?

- Longer depreciation lives
- One-off profits from the sales of office buildings, etc.
- Restructuring charges
- Accelerated recognition of revenues and deferral of costs
- Reversals of a reserve
- Sharp falls in inventories
- Unrecorded stock option plans

Shortcuts: EVA analysis

One shortcut to discovering whether an industry or company is adding value and making profits is Economic Value Added or EVA analysis. *Fortune* magazine describes it as 'today's hottest financial idea and getting hotter'. EVA basically says that a company is creating value for its owners (shareholders) only when its operating income exceeds the cost of the capital employed to make the income happen. This is a powerful

> Today's hottest financial idea and getting hotter.

linkage since of course the owners could invest their capital somewhere else to get a better return.

EVA sews all this up into some nice simple numbers which allow you to compare companies and sectors. Unfortunately, according to Merrill Lynch, the companies making the most EVA are not always the ones the market recognizes with better share prices.[15] Joel M. Stern, the inventor of EVA, countermands that EVA is useful because it shows up companies that are not undertaking new investments which return more than the cost of the capital.

CORPORATE EVENTS:
MERGERS, TAKEOVERS AND IPOs

Corporate events come along with surprising frequency and raise a number of obvious questions. What price is the right takeover premium and are IPOs worth investing in?

Mergers and acquisitions occur for a wide variety of reasons, some meritable and some not. The prime argument is usually synergy. There may be operating economies or pooling of resources that would not otherwise occur if the two companies remained separate. Examples are the merger of Lotus Development Corporation and IBM and the merger of Glaxo and SmithKline Beecham. Other motivations include getting into assets on the cheap (Gulf Oil and Chevron), diversification or tax considerations. Less healthy motives are the desire by management to gain more power and bigger salary packages. Firms may also seek to break up the acquisition and extract value from the parts greater than the cost.

The evidence is that a hostile takeover will merit a 30 per cent increase in the stock price, while a friendly merger will cause a 20 per cent leap.[16] Studies of the long-term benefit for the acquirer are rather less conclusive. Anecdotally in the UK it is obvious that many of the takeover vehicles of the 1980s, including Hanson, BTR and Tomkins, failed to benefit in the long run from their acquisition sprees.

On IPOs we should first be suspicious of the reason behind the decision to come to the stock market. Is the management just dressing up a run of the mill company to cash in their options? Are they seeking to take advantage of excessive market optimism about their sector? Do they really need the cash and is the investment project worthwhile?

IPOs are difficult to price, given that shares have not traded before and the company may have many unique features. Brokers are also understandably concerned that the issue be seen as a success. These factors lead IPOs to be issued at a discount to the real value. According to one source the average underpricing is of the order of 15 per cent.[17] But the evidence is that most of the profits from IPO companies accrue on the first day of trading and sadly most of the stock available is allocated to the big institutions. Other investors acquiring after the first day do not experience abnormal returns.

SUMMARY AND CONCLUSION

In a freely traded share or commodity the price takes into account all known facts. So please do not confuse me with the fundamentals. (*Sri on the Interactive Investor bulletin boards, April 2001*)

The key thing to remember is that, if you use fundamental analysis, you are going to have to take a view. There are no crutches or shortcuts. You need to weigh up the evidence you think is important and come to an independent conclusion. There are of course a number of helpful tools. You can buy into services such as Hemmington Scott or Standard & Poor's that summarize the factual information on a company and make decisions on it. You can use tipsheets and independent sources of information such as websites.

By far the most obvious solution is to use broker reports and let the brokers do the legwork, assembling all the relevant industry and stock specific information. However, a word on brokers is needed. First, brokers do not produce research out of charitable concern for the plight of bewildered private investors. They are part of investment banks designed to maximize profits. Of analysts Warren Buffett warned: 'Never ask a barber if you need a haircut.'

> Of analysts Warren Buffett warned: 'Never ask a barber if you need a haircut.'

The two problems are first that they may withhold sell recommendations and exaggerate the attractiveness of investments to help their corporate finance departments win clients among the companies they are analyzing. According to one fund manager, 'The notion that analysts make independent forecasts is a convenient fiction that suits all parties.'[18]

Second, analysts will be part of investment banks which take positions in the stocks they analyze. So if they are short or long of a stock the analyst might be pressured to make a recommendation convenient to the bank.

On the other hand we should not forget that analysts work at the crux of the information food chain. They may get a bad press, particularly technology stock analysts, but they are generally very strong on detailed industry knowledge and contacts.

What turns the professionals on?

We would expect fund managers to know best. After all, their job it is to deal with flows of competing investment prospects all day long so they ought to know how to sift stocks better than the rest of us. Tony Golding, in *The City: Inside the Great Expectation Machine*, usefully summarized the kinds of things fund managers love and loathe into hard and soft categories. Positives include solid numbers, simple company structures focused on one activity, a memorable story and obvious quality characteristics. Softer factors relate to the credibility of managers, PR and strategy.

Investors like to see solid financial numbers and ratios showing growth of sales and margins, preferably double-digit growth. Investors hate to see such numbers distorted by acquisitions that are dilutive or make the numbers deteriorate. On the other hand acquisitions that are earnings enhancing are greeted with applause. Investors in the UK prefer to see a simple company structure without the confusing crossholdings common in Europe. They like a company focused on a core business so that fund managers can get pure exposure to an exciting area of operations. Stories that make the company memorable will stand out in a fund manager's crowded mind and allow it to be categorized in the market with a 'turnaround' or 'restructuring' label.

Companies benefit by linking into the world of existing blue-chip stocks in fund manager portfolios. They do this by boasting of their blue-chip clients or a key contract with a fashionable name. Companies that can be regarded as commodity businesses are a major turn-off for fund managers. They favour unique businesses with repeatable long-term earning streams or unexploited growth industries.

The key soft factor identified by Golding is the quality of management. Since the management are the face of the company to the all-important institutional investors, their credibility and personality is key. Institutions make judgements about whether to buy on the management promises and sell if they do not deliver. Management also vocalize the strategy and explain it to the investors. How well they and the rest of the company's PR machine do that job can impact the rating of the share price.

So what makes a good stock? This is in the eye of the beholder. You need to be comfortable with both the industry and the stock. Above all you need to be convinced not only about the underlying company, but also that the valuation meets your measure of cheapness. Let's just summarize the conclusions for this section (Table 3.2).

Table 3.2   Indications of industry and company health

What makes a good industry?	What makes a good company?
Positive market growth trends	Exposed to industry growth
Lots of potential markets as yet unexploited	Able to fund its growth
Dynamic product cycles	Management switched on
Healthy but not excessive competition	Good products
Costs contained	Unexploited markets
Suppliers not too powerful	Gearing not excessive
	Valuation comparisons favourable

NOTES

1   In John Train, *Money Masters* (HarperCollins, New York, 2000), p. 122.

2   Benjamin Graham and David Dodd, *Security Analysis: Principals and Techniques* (McGraw-Hill, New York, 1934).

3   Fred Wellings, 'Profits forecasting: a practitioner's view', *Professional Investor*, October (1998), p. 28.

4   Robert C. Higgins, *Analysis for Financial Management*, 6th edn, (McGraw-Hill, Maidenhead, 2001), p. 115.

5   Jonathan Davis, *Money Makers* (Orion, London, 1998), p. 168.

6   A study using the period 1982–9 was originally used to justify this effect but more recent studies undertaking annual rebalancing have not been supportive. Frank Reilly and Dominic Marshall, 'Using P/E/growth ratios to select stocks', (University of Notre Dame, Paris, January 1999).

7   Tom Copeland and Vladimir Antikarov, *Real Options, A Practitioners' Guide* (Texere, New York, 2001, p. 262).

8   George Soros, *The Alchemy of Finance* (Simon and Schuster, New York, 1987), p. 47.

9   John Maynard Keynes said, 'A speculator is one who runs risks of which he is aware and an investor is one who runs risks of which he is unaware.' *The Collected Works of John Maynard Keynes*, Donald Moggridge, ed., Vol. XII (Cambridge University Press, New York, 1983), p. 109. With permission of Palgrave.

10 Jeffrey C. Hooke, *Security Analysis on Wall Street: A Comprehensive Guide to Today's Valuation Methods* (Wiley, New York, 1998), pp. 79–108.

11 Chris Gasson, *Media Equities Evaluation and Trading* (Woodhead Publishing, Cambridge, 1995), p. 4.

12 Nick Antill and Robert Arnott, *Valuing Oil and Gas Companies*, 2nd edn (Woodhead Publishing, Cambridge, 2000), pp. 110–18.

13 Andrew D. Porter and Karen Beynon, *Valuing Chemical Companies*, 2nd edn (Woodhead Publishing, Cambridge, 2000).

14 Charles Kernot, *Valuing Mining Companies*, 2nd edn (Woodhead Publishing, Cambridge, 1999), pp. 156–8.

15 Issued by Merrill Lynch, Pierce, Fenner and Smith, *Merrill Lynch Quantitative Viewpoint: An Analysis of EVA*, by Richard Bernstein and Carmen Pigler, London, 19 December 1997.

16 Michael C. Jensen and Richard S. Ruback, 'The market for corporate control: the scientific evidence', *Journal of Financial Economics*, April (1983), pp. 5–50.

17 B.M. Neuberger and C.A. Lachapelle, 'Unseasoned new issue price performance on three tiers: 1975–80', *Financial Management*, 12, 3 (1983), pp. 23–8.

18 Tony Golding, *The City: Inside The Great Expectations Machine* (Pearson Education, London, 2001), p. 62.

4

Technical analysis

What is technical analysis?

Let's start with the basics

Volume and the Dow Theory

Support and resistance levels

Breakouts and moving averages

Candlesticks

Point and figure charts

Easy patterns to detect

Triangles

Rectangles

Flags

Reversal trends: double tops and head and shoulders

Mathematical indicators

Relative strength indicators (RSI)

Rate of change (ROC) indicators of velocity

MACD

Bollinger bands

Fibonacci retracements

Elliott waves

Market indicators

Contrarian technical analysis rules

Breadth of market indicators

Kondratieff and Coppock

Buy and sell signals

Indicator tips

Many sceptics, it is true, are inclined to dismiss the whole procedure [chart reading] as akin to astrology or necromancy; but the sheer weight of its importance in Wall Street requires that its pretensions be examined with some degree of care. (Benjamin Graham and David L. Dodd)[1]

Those who cannot remember the past are condemned to repeat it. (George Santayana)[2]

WHAT IS TECHNICAL ANALYSIS?

Technical analysis is really about two simple things. The first thing is the *trend* in a stock price. Chartists do not believe that share prices move randomly. The second is the *pattern* in the price chart. Whereas fundamental analysis uses information such as the company's earnings or the state of the economy, technical analysts believe that the market itself is its own best forecaster. They think that prices move in repetitive patterns that provide a visual representation of the market psychology. If this seems hocuspocus to you it is worth bearing in mind that at the very least they have relevance because a significant body of investors think they do.

Technical analysts maintain that the prices and volumes of share trades contain all the meaning you need to arrive at buy and sell decisions. They see things solely in terms of demand and supply. The market is the sum of all rational and irrational influences. Change for technicians does not occur suddenly but in a trend. So they do not accept that information is gobbled up by the market and prices change to prevent profits. They consider that prices move sedately in one direction or the other. They are interested just as much in the change in the rate of change as in the direction. Once a trend develops, rather like a car changing between different gears, it has different levels. They aim to

> **P**rices move in repetitive patterns that provide a visual representation of the market psychology.

identify shifts in the persistence of a trend and believe that trends persist for long times.

We should not confuse this with trends and patterns that appear commonly in fundamental analysis, such as rising sales growth or falling interest rates. Every investor and analyst will also have a mental framework of patterns that he has seen in past industry cycles or events. The difference between fundamental and technical analysis is that technicians see prices as predictable by looking at the past price evidence alone.

Arguments against technical analysis

Some critics argue that price patterns have become self-fulfilling prophecies. For example, let's assume that technicians think a stock will rise to 100 if it breaks through a resistance line at 75, (we will examine these terms shortly). If it does go to 75 *the sheer volume of trades generated by the technicians themselves* will cause the stock to go to 100. Another problem is that if one rule or the other is successful, investors will adopt it in droves and neutralize the value of the technique.

The major studies against technical analysis are the tests for efficient markets. One set of tests analyzed prices to determine whether they were random – a random walk. The second set of tests looked at whether a buy and hold strategy would be better than following trading rules. They found that share prices were indeed a random walk and that a buy and hold strategy outperformed trading. In fact there is a surprising lack of academic evidence in favour of technical analysis. We won't let that stop us here because if enough people believe in something it is bound to influence the behaviour of prices. And lots of people do believe. Here a few justifications from users of the Ample Interactive Investor website:

> Every tipster has some hidden objective. You simply don't know who to believe. Charts are impartial. They work particularly well in a world of mass-market manipulation and market abuse. Long live the chartists! (*Richard Scarlett*)

> Technical Analysis is the only logical way to make decisions that can be backtested on when to buy and sell. It works on any market and any timescale. (*Mike Alexander*)

> Technical Analysis (TA) is merely a consensus accepted by insiders. It does not follow any real flow being only supported by itself. It is a more complicated version of herd following. (*Frederick Mole*)

In order to provide a balanced account it is only fair to include a couple of doubters too:

> All Technical Analysts have 20/20 hindsight but not a Scooby Doo about the future – they would be as well gutting a chicken and reading the entrails! (*Tom Watson*)

> Following charts is for those who like playing with crayons rather than engaging in considered analysis. Of course if we all did charts it would be a self-fulfilling prophecy in the short term. (*Nick Beart*)

Advantages of technical analysis

First, it is quicker to arrive at trading signals than the laborious process of fundamental analysis. Technical analysts claim superior ability to time trades and benefit from getting in low and getting out high. Second, it is less vulnerable to the clever accounting tricks that plague ratio analysis.

LET'S START WITH THE BASICS

We all remember the graph paper with boxes which we used at school for drawing elaborate shapes and bar charts of class heights and weights. This is the starting point of any technical analysis. If you plot the highest and lowest price for a particular day onto the chart and join them up you will have a *range*. The bars representing the daily ranges build up over time to result in a bar chart, a classic charting tool.

Figure 4.1 shows a close-up of a bar chart with the day's high/low and close indicated as a tag. Below the chart you can see the volume shaded to show the direction of the price.

Under the bar chart, it is the convention to put a bar chart of the day's volume over the corresponding period. In order to compress the chart and remove the illusion that a price goes up faster and faster as it rises higher, a special scale is used to scale down the jaggedness of changes over time (logarithmic paper). It allows for better trend and pattern analysis. You will need to select appropriate timescales to work with. The longer the timescale, the wider your horizon to spot trends and patterns.

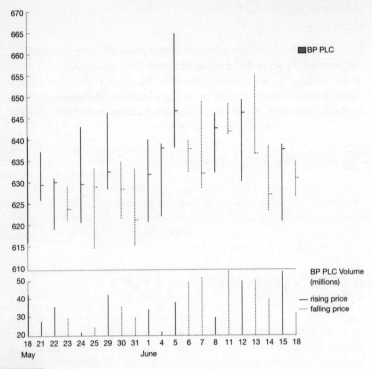

Figure 4.1 Bar chart

Source: Interactive Investor International (now Ample.com) 2001. Reproduced with permission of Ample Interactive Investor. All Rights Reserved.

VOLUME AND THE DOW THEORY

The price change alone does not tell us all we need to know. The volume of stock traded *confirms* the trend. An increase on heavy volume is a positive signal, while a price decline on heavy volume is bearish. English technical analysts used to pay less attention to volume than US technicians, who were influenced by Charles Dow, the founder of the famous *Wall Street Journal* and the Dow Jones Index. Dow described stock prices as moving in three types of trends analogous to the movements of water:

● major trends like the huge tides of an ocean

- middling tides that resemble waves
- short run movements like ripples.

Followers of the Dow Theory recognize that prices do not go straight up, but occasionally go in the opposite direction. Technicians also use a ratio of the volume traded of rising shares to the volume traded of falling shares to indicate the overall *momentum* of a market. This is reported daily in publications such a such as the *Wall Street Journal* and *Financial Times*.

SUPPORT AND RESISTANCE LEVELS

Once you have got your chart you can draw on a *trendline*. You may prefer to work with an ordinary line graph, shown in Figure 4.2, rather than use the daily highs and lows. The extreme bumps in the price chart, the

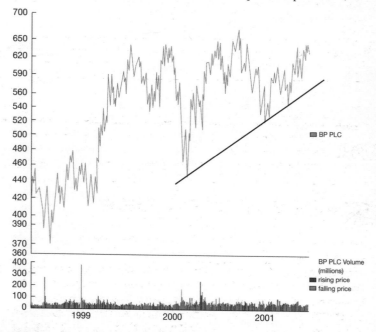

Figure 4.2 An upward trend line drawn on top of a line graph for BP (log scale)

Source: Interactive Investor International (now Ample.com) 2001. Reproduced with permission of Ample Interactive Investor. All Rights Reserved.

highs and lows will tell you where to put the trendline. You should take care that your trendline has more than two points of contact with the low or high points you are illustrating. A technical analyst will believe that a trend will continue for a long time. So once your trendline is established, the strategy is to buy on the dips if the trend is upward guided by your trendline and sell on the rises if your trendline is downward.

A *support level* is the price range at which the technician expects demand for the stock to increase. Investors are snapping up stock at lower prices. Technicians believe that if a stock has been rising and then falls slightly, it will hit a support level as all of those investors left out of the rise rush to get into the stock.

A *resistance level* is a price range where an increase in the supply of stock will occur on a price rise leading to a rapid reversal of any price gain. People are selling into higher prices. A resistance level is more likely to occur after a stock has steadily declined from a higher level. A supply of stock is said to be overhanging the market.

BREAKOUTS AND MOVING AVERAGES

It is easy enough to understand the concept of an average. The average of days in a week is seven. But a moving average may take a while to get your head around. Let's say that instead of seven days, this week happened to have fourteen. The moving average over the past two weeks is therefore no longer seven days in the average week but 10.5.

A moving average in a share price keeps track of the change in the average share price over a defined time period. The most commonly used short- and long-term moving averages are the 50-day and 200-day moving averages. It just adds up the share price for those 50 or 200 most recent days and divides by 50 or 200. This number will change over time, lagging the movement in the current share price.

It makes sense that an average will trail the trend if the price is rising, and in a falling market the average will be above the current price. It is usual for chartists to overlay two moving averages – a short and a longer period moving average. If the price begins to slow down or go into reverse, then the moving average covering the shorter period will go down first. A shorter moving average is obviously a lot more volatile than a longer one (Figure 4.3).

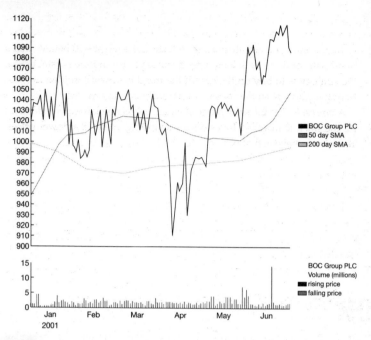

Figure 4.3 Diagram of a line graph (log scale) with 50-day and 200-day moving average crossing over

Source: Interactive Investor International (now Ample.com) 2001. Reproduced with permission of Ample Interactive Investor. All Rights Reserved.

When the shorter moving average slows first, it is possible that it will *cross over* the longer average. This is considered significant if and only if both moving averages are moving in the same direction as each other. In the event that both moving averages were rising when the crossover happened, this is a bullish signal called a Golden Cross. If the moving averages are both heading down, this is a bearish signal called a Bearish Cross. Both of these are regarded as indicating a change in the overall trend. When a 50-day moving average crosses the 200-day from below on high volume, this signals a reversal from negative to positive. On the contrary, if a 50-day moving average crosses a 200-day line from above, then this is considered a sell indicator. As always, the technical analyst will look to volume to support the conclusion.

If prices *break out* through a trend line, chartists consider this significant if accompanied by heavy volume. For instance, if a stock price reverses, a trend breaks through a moving average from below having been trending down and if accompanied by strong trading volume this is considered a positive sign.

CANDLESTICKS

These originated in Japan and are referred to as candlesticks because of the shape of the plot, which looks like a little candle. They are plotted using the day's high and low like a bar chart. However, if the closing price of the day was above the opening price, then the box is left empty. If the price closed lower than it opened, then the box is filled in.

The vocabulary of candlesticks is one of oriental names attributing meaning to the various colour patterns that are produced. Chartists see significance in the length of the candle. A long black body is a bearish signal, while a long white body is a positive signal. Short candlesticks, *dojis*, where the price at open and close was similar can be seen as significant, forming tops and bottoms of a trend (Figure 4.4).

POINT AND FIGURE CHARTS

Technical analysts don't just use bar charts; they also use the strangely named point and figure charts. In these charts the price changes that are too small to register are omitted and the timescale is also left out. A rising price is represented by an X and a falling price by an O. The chart is plotted in vertical columns and only changes if the price moves outside the box in which it was last plotted. The chartist determines which movements are significant enough to be registered.

For example, if you decided only to record changes of more than 4 and the stock price started at 40 and moved to 42, you would record an X in the box above 40 and do nothing else until the stock rose above 44 or dropped below 38 (a four-point reversal from its high of 42). If it dropped to 38, you would move the column to the right, indicating the direction of movement had changed, and put an O to indicate a decline to 38. If the price dropped another 4 points you add another O. Only if it moves

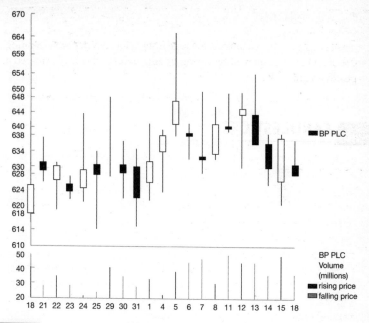

Figure 4.4 Diagram of a candlestick chart for BP

Source: Interactive Investor International (now Ample.com) 2001. Reproduced with permission of Ample Interactive Investor. All Rights Reserved.

another four points in the opposite direction would you move to the next column and begin again with an X. Over time you will plot what looks very like a bar chart and trendlines and breakouts can be detected.

Technicians favour point and figure charts because they screen out the irrelevant sideways movements and present changes in trends starkly.

EASY PATTERNS TO DETECT

A great deal of technical analysis concerns the ability to spot constantly repeated patterns. This is where technical analysis overlaps with human psychology. We can all recognize well-established patterns of constantly repeated behaviour. In technical analysis such patterns will last differing lengths of time and arise with different degrees of strength.

TRIANGLES

One of the easiest and most common patterns to detect is the triangle pattern typical of a rising market. Triangles indicate a battle going on between buyers and sellers. They can be formed from a horizontal line on top and a line below the rising share price. They can have flat tops or in a market trending sideways they might have more of a '>' shape. A flat-topped triangle arises because the price is hitting resistance at a particular level and sellers are coming in at that point. At some point the buyers will gain the upper hand and the ceiling of the triangle will rise. The pattern is most certain when there are more than a couple of points of contact on the top and bottom lines. Uncertainty will be more likely close to the apex. Target prices can be deduced from the depth of the triangle (Figure 4.5).

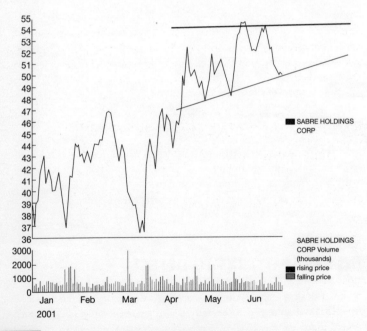

| Figure 4.5 | Diagram of a triangle pattern overlaid onto a chart |

Source: Interactive Investor International (now Ample.com) 2001. Reproduced with permission of Ample Interactive Investor. All Rights Reserved.

RECTANGLES

This shape is rather less common than the triangle. It occurs when a stock is trending up and down within a narrow range, the bounds of which can be drawn as two lines (hence the rectangle name) on a couple of contact points to the extreme highs and lows of the share price. What this is saying is that there is a fairly undecided argument going on between buyers and sellers. When one or other becomes exhausted, the price moves swiftly up or down through the bounds, although it might temporarily pull back. Rectangles can build up over a couple of months and may not resolve themselves for many months more.

FLAGS

These formations occur in fast-moving situations. Basically they occur when a rising or falling stock price stalls. They are compacted miniature consolidations in a sharp upward or downward movement. Because the rise or fall is so steep, they look like flagpoles – hence the name of flags for these formations.

REVERSAL TRENDS: DOUBLE TOPS AND HEAD AND SHOULDERS

Two of the most common reversal patterns – double tops and head and shoulders – can be described in terms of investor psychology.

Double tops

Double tops occur when the market hits a peak, then sells off, then rallies up to the old peak and then falls again. So the price chart looks like the letter M. The mid-point of the M pattern is the support point. In terms of investor behaviour, this can be seen as investors initially being reluctant to accept that the high prices are wrong and chasing the share back up after its first fall. After a while though, the sellers gain the upper hand and force the price to 'double top' and fall. The complete opposite of a double top is a double bottom where the chart looks like the letter W. In this case the buyers eventually gain the upper hand and the price rises. Both are regarded as powerful signals, but are very rare indeed.

Head and shoulders

A more common occurrence is the head and shoulders formation (Figure 4.6). This pattern builds up when a price has been in an upward trend for some time and lots of investors are in heavy profit. The pattern develops out of three peaks. The top of the inner peak (the head) must be higher than the two outer peaks (the shoulders). In terms of demand and supply, the reason the shoulders form is that investors are inclined to take profits

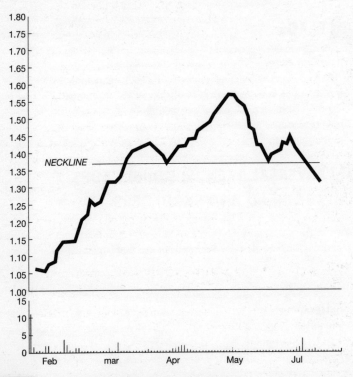

Figure 4.6 **Example of a head and shoulders formation**

around that plateau and when the price fails to break through the higher peak (the head) it settles back to the old familiar level as before, forming the second shoulder. If the price breaks through the neckline, this is regarded as a serious negative signal. In a bear market the exact opposite of a head and shoulders can form and any breakout through the upside down shoulders is then regarded as a very positive signal.

MATHEMATICAL INDICATORS

Technical analysts do not produce charts full of flashy indicators just to show off. Indicators are simply a mechanism for cutting down on the margin of error. Computing power has increased the usage of complex indicators of all kinds, but the object always remains the same – to refine the signals and reduce the error.

RELATIVE STRENGTH INDICATORS (RSI)

The relative part of the relative strength indicators refers to comparison with the market. It works out how your share is performing relative to everyone else so that you can see whether you are falling behind or getting ahead. Technicians believe that a trend of underperforming or outperforming the market will continue and that the trends (in this trend) can be charted just like any other.

Technicians therefore compute weekly or monthly relative strength ratios, for instance, for a stock or for an industry group. They are computed relative to some index such as the S&P 400 or the FTSE 100. Relative strength indices work during rising as well as falling markets. A positive relative strength in combination with moving average lines crossing is a powerful buy signal. A change in the trend of relative strength can be a strong buy or sell signal, particularly if confirmed by successive lurches in the RSI up or down (Figure 4.7).

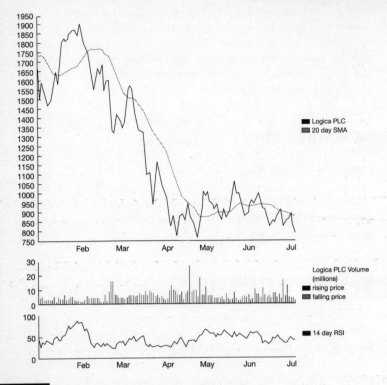

Figure 4.7 **Example of a relative strength indicator (RSI)**

Source: Interactive Investor International (now Ample.com) 2001. Reproduced with permission of Ample Interactive Investor. All Rights Reserved.

RATE OF CHANGE (ROC)
INDICATORS OF VELOCITY

This measure is calculated over a short time period such as 14 days and is a measure of the momentum or velocity of the change. It indicates whether the price has moved too far too fast or is speeding up. Generally this is worked out as a percentage of 100, with numbers above 50 indicating overbought and below 50 indicating oversold. It is rarely used on its own, but rather for confirmation of other trends. To calculate the ROC, you divide the latest closing price by the closing price the desired number

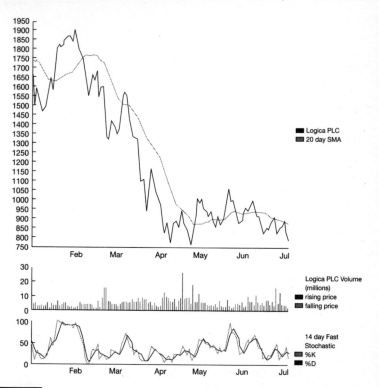

Figure 4.8 **Example of a velocity indicator**

Source: Interactive Investor International (now Ample.com) 2001. Reproduced with permission of Ample Interactive Investor. All Rights Reserved.

of days ago then multiply by 100. This value is then used as the 'reference line' (the 'K' line). A smoothed version of this line (a 'D' line) can then be monitored for crossovers (Figure 4.8).

MACD

What is it? This is the moving average convergence/divergence indicator – or MACD for short. As we know, moving average lines are constantly moving relative to each other, either towards or away from each other and even crossing each other. The moving average convergence/divergence

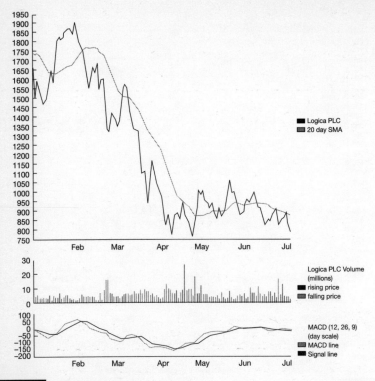

Figure 4.9 **An example of MACD**

Source: Interactive Investor International (now Ample.com) 2001. Reproduced with permission of Ample Interactive Investor. All Rights Reserved.

indicator measures the extent of this convergence or divergence. If two moving averages are the same, then the MACD is given a value of zero. If the shorter term moving average goes above the longer term MA, the difference is a positive value. When the shorter term moving average falls below the longer term then this is plotted as a negative value (Figure 4.9).

BOLLINGER BANDS

These were developed by John Bollinger who went on to found a successful fund trading on the principle that the volatility of a share price (its

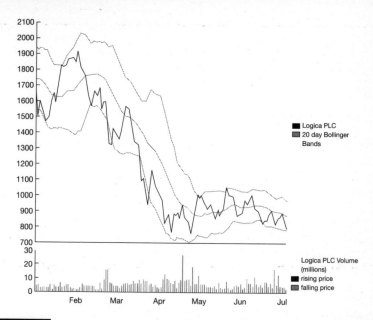

Figure 4.10 An example of Bollinger bands

Source: Interactive Investor International (now Ample.com) 2001. Reproduced with permission of Ample Interactive Investor. All Rights Reserved.

standard deviation in mathematical terms) should form bands above and below the actual share price. In a very jumpy market the bands will be wide. In a flat market the bands will narrow.

It is said to be significant when the share price breaks through the band. This will often signal the start of a trend. Other indicators such as RSI should confirm this. A 20-day average with two 'standard deviations' is popular for short and medium term analysis. For longer periods a 50-day average with 2.5 standard deviations may be better, while shorter periods will find 10-day moving averages and one standard deviation sufficient (Figure 4.10).

FIBONACCI RETRACEMENTS

A standard stock market pattern is where a move in one direction is followed by a retracement in the opposite direction. Technical analysts, believing that markets are predictable, will try and predict these retracements. They have dug up Leonardo Fibonacci, an Italian mathematician whose technique was to build up a sequence of numbers in which each previous number is the sum of the two previous numbers, 0,1,1,2,3,5,8,13,21 etc.

Buried in this series of numbers is the Golden Mean, which is the ratio between any two successive numbers in the sequence. It works out at about 61.8 per cent and is one of those numbers that crops up all over the place. The Greeks knew about it and called it phi. The Nautilus shell (*Nautilus pompilius*) grows larger on each spiral by phi.

The sunflower has 55 clockwise spirals overlaid on either 34 or 89 counter-clockwise spirals, a phi proportion. It also crops up in music and architecture.

In charts it seems that many retracements cease at 38.2 per cent on the way down leaving 61.8 per cent of the price intact. It is difficult to know why this might be so other than that lots of investors believe that this is the case.

ELLIOTT WAVES

Ralph Nelson Elliott observed more than half a century ago that stock market movements unfold in a series of rhythmic patterns based on a natural shifts in investor mood. In Elliott's own words:

> Practically all developments which result from [human] social-economic processes follow a law that causes them to repeat themselves in similar and constantly recurring serials of waves or impulses of definite number and pattern.[3]

Elliott believed that waves occur in three parts, a riding impulse wave of five parts followed by a corrective wave of three parts, with the relationship between them determined by various rules such as Fibonacci numbers. Corrective wave or retracements would typically be 38.2 per cent. Underlying the Elliott wave theory is the basic assumption of a long-term bull market in which there is a regular compounding accrual with occasional setbacks quantifiable as phi, 38.2 per cent.

MARKET INDICATORS

Many technical analysts pay great attention to indicators that are reckoned to foreshadow events elsewhere in the market. Commodity prices are seen by some technicians as giving advance warning of changes or trends in the world economy. Although some individual commodities such as oil are closely followed, indexes of a number of commodities bundled together are normally used. An example is the Bridge Commodity Research Bureau futures index, traded in New York.

Other chartists prefer to look at different leading indicators. Commodities may actually lag the movement of the economy as suppliers build up capacity during the boom and regret it during a downswing, building up stocks rather than mothballing capacity.

CONTRARIAN TECHNICAL ANALYSIS RULES

Many technical analysts have developed trading rules based on a contrarian notion that the majority of investors are wrong as the market approaches peaks and troughs. If a technician can identify a peak or trough, then he can trade in the opposite direction.

The level of cash held by fund managers is one such indicator of a market approaching its peak or trough. If fund managers are bullish, then they will have used up all their cash to buy stocks, and if bearish they will be holding lots of cash. The level of cash held by private investors is a statistic that is available from adding up cash in brokerage accounts. A decline in cash balances indicates a fall in available buying power and is a bearish signal, while higher cash balances are a bullish sign.

The put/call ratio is one more such rule designed to spot market trends. If there are more outstanding call options (the option/right to buy stocks) than there are put options (the option/right to sell stocks), then that is a bearish sign indicating excessive bullishness.

BREADTH OF MARKET INDICATORS

Technical analysts also pay close attention to market statistics such as daily highs and lows and the number of issues rising and falling. A technician would look for a highs/lows ratio or an advances/decliners ratio to show a divergence from the trend in the main general index of the market. That could indicate underlying trends changing.

KONDRATIEFF AND COPPOCK

Very long run indicators

If you accept the importance of trends then this applies over all time periods, not only the short run. Kondratieff, working in Russia in the 1920s, traced a 54-year cycle in the peaks to troughs of interest rates. He set out evidence of a cycle of interest rates using bond yields as a proxy for rates. He then used grain prices to show parallel trends in the wider economy through wars and other political and social developments. For Kondratieff, a cycle is set off by major innovations such as the railroads or the automobile.

One rationalization is that cycles can reflect opposing cultural attitudes of subsequent generations. Another is that technological advances such as railways, motor cars and computers regularly come along and mop up spare capital, driving interest rates up. In the UK, for example, interest rates started to rise in 1946 and peaked in 1974–5. They have been falling more or less in a straight line to the present day. Since interest rates reflect demand and supply of loans to invest on a global basis, the rate may have significance in many areas. In the USA there is a similar interest rate cycle to the UK.

Yet another long run indicator is the Coppock indicator which is featured in publications such as the *Investor's Chronicle*. This is based on a mechanical system devised by Edwin Coppock, a Texan investor. The buy indicator is a function of three consecutive similar monthly changes in the direction of the indicator.

BUY AND SELL SIGNALS

The object of technical analysis is really to provide buy and sell signals, to simplify stock market investment into a set of rules. A technical analyst is hoping to benefit from the major part of trends that have been identified.

Whether or not you accept the validity of technical analysis, it is important to understand the signals by which technical analysis works. Technical analysts will often overlay indicators and seek out confirmatory signals. The summary signals list that follows is by no means complete, but serves as an indication of what technical analysts are actually up to.

> The object of technical analysis is really to provide buy and sell signals, to simplify stock market investment into a set of rules.

Buy signals

- If the moving average line flattens following a decline and the price of the stock penetrates that moving average line on the upside, this constitutes a major buying signal.
- When the 50-day moving average breaks through the 200-day moving average, this is a significant event. If the 50-day moving average breaks through heading up, this is a positive signal.
- If the price of the stock falls below the moving average line while the moving average line is still going up, you should buy the stock.
- If the stock price travels above the moving average but bounces off it when it dips lower and instead turns up again, this is a buying signal.
- If the stock price falls too violently below a declining moving average line, a rebound is likely.

Sell signals

- If the moving average line flattens or declines following a rise, and the stock price penetrates that line heading down, this constitutes an important selling signal.
- When the 50-day moving average breaks through the 200-day moving average, this is a significant event. If the 50-day moving average breaks through heading down, this is a negative signal.
- A sell signal is given if the stock price rises above the moving average line while the average line is still going down.
- If the stock price has difficulty penetrating the moving average then that too is a sell signal, particularly after a number of a failed attempts to penetrate.

- Where the share price spikes up above the moving average line it may have moved too far too fast and will probably head back down.

INDICATOR TIPS

- Multiple indicators give more valid signals than individual indicators.
- Indicators are useful to confirm that a change in the trend has taken place.
- Momentum can be detected using indicators such as RSI, MACD and Bollinger bands.
- MACD works well in both a trending market and a market trading in a volatile trading range.
- Watch out for the signal line crossing over the MACD line.
- RSI is more reliable in a trending market.
- Bollinger bands will tighten in a flat market so a breakout will be signalled early.

NOTES

1   Benjamin Graham and David L. Dodd, *Security Analysis: Principles and Techniques* (McGraw-Hill, New York, 1934).
2   George Santayana, *Life of Reason* (1905–6), Chapter 12.
3   R.N. Elliott, *Nature's Law: The Secret of the Universe* (1946), reprinted in *R.N. Elliott's Masterworks: The Definitive Collection*, ed. Robert R. Prechter (McGraw-Hill, Dubuque, IA, 1994).

5

A more professional portfolio

Common stock purchases obtained through purchases month-by-month, at low prices as well as high, would have provided a very effective method of investing a portion of retirement funds. Most of the difficulties in individual investing in equities arise from lack of diversification both among shares and over time. (William C Greenough)[1]

The greatest safety lies in putting all your eggs in one basket and watching the basket. (Gerald M Loeb)[2]

STEP 1:
YOUR PORTFOLIO AND YOUR NEEDS

Once you have decided to build a portfolio you will need to ask yourself a number of questions to manage it professionally.

- You need to establish what are your *goals and objectives*.
- You need to establish a *time horizon*, how long you want to hold onto your investments.
- You need to work out your *risk level and expectations*.

Because of changes in your commitments and your assets over time, your investment strategy will change over your life.

The early stage, say up to your mid-thirties, will involve the *accumulation* of assets. There will be short-term needs such as saving for a down payment on a house, holidays or car and then there will be longer term needs such as establishing a pension or saving for your children's education. Because of the long-term time horizon, you will be able to take on higher risk investments in the hope of making good gains.

> Because of changes in your commitments and your assets over time, your investment strategy will change over your life.

Between your mid-thirties and your fifties you will be in the *consolidation* phase of your investment strategy. You may be at your career peak and earning a good salary. You may have paid off most of your mortgage. You may still have some commitments to pay your children's college bills, but these are coming to an end. You will have a surplus to save and invest. Since your time horizon is still quite long, moderately risky investments will be most satisfactory. An increasing concern though will be capital preservation, as you do not want to put your capital at risk.

A final lifecycle phase is your *retirement* when you are spending the accumulated assets. Living expenses are covered by social security and pensions. The important thing in this stage is to protect against the effects of inflation, not forgetting that retirement on average lasts around 20 years. You may initially wish just to preserve capital while drawing down a rising income. Completely different types of investments are required to accomplish this goal compared to previous strategies.

Your portfolio

You will need to work out an investment strategy that offers the most suitable way forward. You should first consider your tolerance to risk, your investment goals and any constraints such as your tax status or obligations to fund a child through college.

What is your investment goal – to make a lot of money? This is the obvious answer but is probably not suitable for most investors. The fact is that the market is very volatile. It can go up and down by 10 per cent in a day (or even 22 per cent on Wall Street's Black Monday in 1987). Individual stocks can go up and down even more. Your portfolio needs to be robust enough to see out likely falls and rises in a volatile investment world, but it also needs to be designed to take advantage of changes in prices of the various assets.

25 years old

At this age your investment goal is likely to be capital gains. If you hold a steady job, you are likely to see income rising. So you should be able to carry high amounts of risk. You can consider higher risk stocks and industries as well as exposure to emerging markets. Income is not a major priority.

45 years old

At this age your investment goal is becoming more conservative. You can still take on some risk, but you are looking for security of your capital and beginning to consider income.

65 years old

At this age your investment focus is on getting income from your assets while preserving both income and capital from the effects of inflation.

The risk quiz

How risk averse are you?

1 You have bought a stock for 100 that has doubled. Do you (a) sell half (b) buy more?
2 You win £100 in the office Christmas draw. Do you (a) pay off your overdrawn cheque account; (b) spend the lot on a riotous evening out?
3 A good description of your attitude to money is (a) save the pennies and the pounds will add up; (b) borrow as much as you can?
4 Your friends would describe you as (a) miserly; (b) always first to pay for a round of drinks?
5 When the stock market takes a tumble, do you (a) buy; (b) sell?
6 I hold stocks (a) for the long run; (b) for fun.
7 My early life was (a) a struggle for security; (b) one long party spending Dad's money?

The more (b)s you score, the less risk averse you are.

Time horizon

There are some obvious constraints on your investing. One is any immediate need for cash. We will assume that these are amply covered by your current account and income. A younger person will clearly have a longer time horizon than someone older and will be able to take on more risk. This does not mean that someone older will have a zero exposure to risk. In order to preserve the real value of capital after inflation, it will be necessary to have some exposure to the stock market.

Taxes and transaction costs

Investment planning is made more difficult by the different tax status of every individual in each country. Specialist advice should always be sought. Purchases and sales will both attract stock brokerage commission and suffer from the bid/offer spread.

In the UK there is still a 0.5 per cent government stamp duty payable on share purchases, so frequent trading will attract additional costs. Many professional equities fund managers buy and sell the equivalent of their whole portfolio once per year.

STEP 2: PICK A BENCHMARK

Your total return will need to be measured in a given time period such as one-quarter year or one year. You should calculate your total value at the beginning and end, including dividends and excluding any contribution of additional capital. Whereas a professional investor would weight the portfolio performance to account for new funds, a private investor might just as well wait until the start of the next quarter to account for new funds.

As we have noted, most people want to make money from their investments. But you are not just trying to make lots of money. You are really trying to beat the market. All those advertisements boasting of how much money you could have made had you invested in a particular fund ten years ago are irrelevant. Indeed at the time of writing the UK's regulatory authority is considering whether to ban them.

> You are not just trying to make lots of money. You are really trying to beat the market.

To determine whether you are beating the market, you need to compare the performance of your investments to a market index or benchmark. If your portfolio consists of the largest US companies, you might choose the Dow Jones Industrial Average. If it were full of big UK stocks, you would choose the FTSE 100. If there are lots of small stocks, you should choose a wider index that covers all shares in the index. There are also special indices for technology and other sectors.

Unfortunately, concentration among large international companies has made for concentration of risk in many indices that are heavily weighted towards oils, pharmaceuticals and telecommunications. These sectors made up 43 per cent of the UK's FTSE 100 index in 2001, up from 26 per cent five years ago.[3] Because of their dominance of the index, you cannot match the index if you avoid these sectors. Many of these sectors are also lacking long-term prospects. So you should be careful to choose an index that matches your portfolio objectives. The other problem with indices is that they are constantly chopping and changing and may need rebalancing, which attracts transaction costs.

STEP 3: UNDERSTAND RISK VS. RETURN

Risk is completely relative to the individual and their circumstances, therefore risk measurements could be very misleading if people don't interpret them properly. (*Mike Embrey on an Interactive Investor bulletin board*)

If I'm walking along a cliff edge on a windy day, I know it's risky, it seems odd to try and put a figure on that, say 457, what? (*Keith Beef on an Interactive Investor bulletin board*)

Measuring risk in your financial affairs is not intuitively obvious. Luckily the two basic premises of portfolio management have been passed on to us from the cradle. First, nobody likes risk. We would much rather avoid it and we get round this by hedging our bets and holding different types of financial assets. We don't put all our eggs in one basket. The constitution of our economy means that high risk is rewarded. A stock market which allows us to take a small part in a big risk oils the wheels of the great economic gamble.

Second, as the tired old saying goes, nothing ventured nothing gained. When things are certain, there won't be a lot of upside. When there is uncertainty, the price you pay now will be low and reflect the possibility of downside. But if things go well it will offer plenty of upside in compensation. These are the basic premises of Modern Portfolio Theory (MPT) which informs the decision making of professional fund managers everywhere today.

As we know, most investors want to make as much money as possible. But of course that does not mean that we should immediately rush out to borrow millions of dollars and speculate in the volatile derivatives markets; nor does it mean that we should buy up the gold supply of Russia in the hope of cornering the world gold market. We want to make the money while avoiding the hazard of losing the lot.

For investors, risk is not just a general negative word as in everyday speech. Risk can be quantified by putting the numbers showing the daily ups and downs of stocks through a model. It can then be used as a tool to increase the returns in your portfolio.

Who is Harry Markowitz and what is Modern Portfolio Theory? Harry B. Markowitz, a graduate student in economics at the University of Chicago, developed the simple principles of 'Nothing ventured, nothing gained' and 'Don't put all your eggs in one basket' into a comprehensive system of diversifying your investments to get an optimal trade-off between risk and reward. In 1990 he was awarded the Nobel Prize in Economics.

If you know the risk for various different stocks and expect some to have better returns than others in a future year, it is a simple step to find the best one to invest in. You want the one with the highest returns to the lowest risk. The winner, according to Modern Portfolio Theory, is the one who can put together the portfolio with the highest returns for the lowest risk, the optimal portfolio that dominates other possible portfolios.[4] If you map out on a graph all the portfolios of risk and return for different investors, many people will be below the optimal point for their level of risk. They will be taking on too much risk for too little return. Some will be above it. If you do your sums and compare the number of stocks to the level of risk, it turns out that risk falls steeply once you have about 10 or 12 stocks in your portfolio (Figure 5.1).

> For investors, risk is not just a general negative word as in everyday speech.

STEP 4:
DESIGNING THE PORTFOLIO UNIVERSE

What is your universe of investments? If we consider all those assets in the world that are easily tradable, the global market portfolio of assets in which we can potentially invest, we find that they add up to a staggering $58 trillion in 1998. US equities amount to 21.7 per cent of the total, Japanese equities make up 4.2 per cent and all other global equities comprise

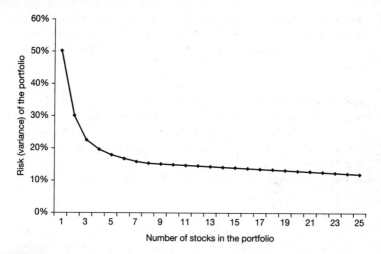

Figure 5.1 The level of variance (risk) in a portfolio falls sharply as you increase the number of stocks in your portfolio from 1 to 10 and varies little once you have 10 or more stocks

Source: Asweth Damodaran, (1996) *Investment Valuation* New York: Wiley, p. 28, Fig 3.5. This material is used by permission of John Wiley & Sons, Inc.

19.6 per cent. Most of the rest of the total, around half, is made up by bond issues. The trend is that non-US assets are growing faster than US assets as a proportion of the total. In fact the US proportion of the stock and bond market has declined from 65 per cent of the total in 1969 to 47 per cent of the total in 1998.

Which bits of the collective wealth of all nations should I invest in? Let's start by defining what there is to invest in. Not long ago, if you went along to your broker or bank manager with money to invest he would recommend a couple of local stocks or perhaps some government bonds. Now technology has made capital mobile. Investment managers, banks and stockbrokers operate globally and 24 hours a day. If you want to, you can buy Japanese bonds, US biotechnology stocks, a British telecom company or a German investment fund all at once. The universe of available investment opportunities is greater than ever before.

Different assets, different risks

OK, so there's a lot of choice, but what about risk? Returns depend on risk, don't they?

Risk in shares

There is no legal reason why you can't lose all your investment in a stock. It is worth focusing on the fact that stocks are really an advance of capital

> ...OK, so there's a lot of choice, but what about risk? Returns depend on risk, don't they? ....

to managers of companies in order to participate in the success of their undertakings. If they are successful, you will benefit. Of course holding a number of stocks in different businesses and opposing industries can rapidly reduce risk. Risk can also be measured against the average risk of

the stock market. If the stock market has a risk of one and you own a stock 20 per cent riskier then you can quantify that risk as 1.2. You can thus decide a target level of risk, which we will discuss in more detail later (page 126).

Risk in bonds and cash

What is a bond? Bills and bonds generally pay a fixed rate of interest. They are a contract promising payment of an unchanging interest rate at set times. Investors who purchase these are really acting as bankers to the borrower. Investors will not get any return other than their coupon and if all goes well the original principal of the bond. Bonds are clearly considerably less variable than equities and so cannot demand much of a return from issuers.

As interest rates rise, the principal value of the bond will fall. Its fixed coupon will be worth less to the buyer who can find high interest rates elsewhere. It will generally fall further for longer maturities such as a 20-year bond than for shorter dated bonds. So you can take on more or less risk depending on your view of which way interest rates are heading.

What is the risk of bonds compared to equities? There is less price volatility in bonds than shares but there is a different kind of risk. As J.M. Keynes pointed out: 'An investment in common stocks is an investment in real values. An investment in a bond is an investment in money values.'[5]

Because of inflation it is money rather than equities which will in the end depreciate in value, giving you less eventual purchasing power. Equities are more likely to offer protection from inflation.

Corporate bonds offer exposure to the risk of the issuer. You might buy the bonds of a distressed company in the hope of an improvement in its circumstances or stick to higher quality issues. In most countries there is also a lively market in debt based on cash flows from mortgages or backed by regional governments or agencies. This will tend to offer a premium interest rate to the one offered by the central government bonds to reflect the added risk of default.

What's this about bonds going down when interest rates go up? It's true! When interest rates go up, all assets with fixed interest rates fall in value. And when rates go down, the opposite occurs.

For cash accounts you deposit money and receive interest and in doing so you lend money to the provider who lends it on to somebody else. Most likely you will have a variable interest rate unlike the fixed interest rate of a bond, so you are exposed to the risk that interest rates might fall. Because the government generally insures savings accounts, there is less risk than bonds and considerably less risk than stocks. For larger amounts certificates of deposit allow access to the interest rates available on the wholesale money markets.

Risk in other assets

The last main class of investments worth mentioning is commodities. Commodities such as gold and palladium do not pay any income and may attract storage costs. Their value will depend on factors such as demand and supply. Risk may depend more on considerations such as liquidity and exchange rates.

Aside from these financial assets there are real assets such as property, art and antiques. Unlike the financial assets, these assets are difficult to price. They may trade infrequently and prices may not be easily discovered. You may enjoy and benefit from living in your

> You may enjoy and benefit from living in your property surrounded by fine art but it will not generate any cash flow and will attract insurance, maintenance and appraisal costs.

property surrounded by fine art but it will not generate any cash flow and will attract insurance, maintenance and appraisal costs. When you sell them, typically at auction, the auction house will demand commission of up to 20 per cent.

STEP 5: BONDS VS. EQUITIES

Which proportion in stocks – the asset allocation decision

Most of the returns over time will not be determined by your decision to invest but by the balance between cash or bonds and risky equities. In other words whether to balance your portfolio in bonds and cash rather than equities is the key decision. If you are seeking capital preservation, you are more likely to hold more bonds than equities.

Typically a growth investor will have a ratio of 70/30 of his portfolio in equities/bonds while an income investor will have 30/70. Another way of doing it is to take 100 and subtract your age. So if like me you are 29 years old, then 100 minus 29 is 71. According to this formula, I should put 71 per cent of my assets into equities and 29 per cent into bonds. One of the most comprehensive studies of the returns of stocks versus other assets is on the UK stock market. A summary of the results is shown in Table 5.1.

Table 5.1 **UK market stocks returns vs. other assets**

UK market returns	1918 value (£)	1999 value (£)	2000) value (£)	2000 return (£)	1918–2000 return (%)	Risk (%)
Nominal						
Equities	100	1,238,492	1,175,288	–5.1	12.1	24.6
Bonds/gilts	100	13,327	14,367	7.8	6.2	13.3
Cash (T bills)	100	7,425	7,887	6.2	5.5	4.2
Real						
Equities	100	58,835	54,259	–7.8	8.0	22.9
Bonds/gilts	100	633	663	4.8	2.3	15.0
Cash (T bills)	100	353	364	3.2	1.6	6.5

Source: Issued by Credit Suisse First Boston (Europe) Ltd, Economics and Equity Research, *2001 Equity Gilt Study* by Robert Barrie, Robert Jukes, Richard Kersley, Anna Mackman CFA, Steve Wright and William Porter, London, April 2001. With permission of Crédit Suisse First Boston.

Table 5.1 shows that between 1918 and 2000 UK equities produced an average real return (after inflation) of 8 per cent per year compared to 2.3 per cent per year for bonds.

Different countries have different preferences

The UK and US are heavily biased towards equities, while Germany generally invests a lower proportion. Institutional investors in the UK invest 72 per cent of assets in equities, in the USA 45 per cent in equities. UK investors are particularly biased against bonds, perhaps because of a history of high inflation, while the USA has developed a lively market in all manner of bonds.

In Germany institutional investors put only 11 per cent of their portfolios into shares. Part of this is due to the average age of the population which is highest in Germany and lower in the USA and UK. Another reason is the ease with which companies in Germany can raise funds from banks rather than the stock market, which is the most common route in the UK and USA. Until quite recently many Germans associated the stock market with gambling and preferred the safety of investing in bonds.

Table 5.2 Typical institutional portfolios: equities vs. bonds

	Bonds	Equities
USA	30	70
UK	20–25	70
Europe	70	30

Source: Tony Golding (2001), *The City: Inside the Great Expectations Machine*, London: Pearson Education, p. 38.

STEP 6: COMBINING SHARES

What is a portfolio? It is simply a diversified group of assets each with different patterns of returns over time.[6] Hopefully the good will balance out the bad. The management of a portfolio can be efficient or inefficient, just like anything else. If you are not careful you can accumulate all sorts of stocks that have no logic to them. There may be stocks you should have sold. After all it is painful to accept you made an investment error; far easier to hope that one day things will turn out right. There may be stocks you have investigated and know you should buy. You ought to regularly ask yourself the question: If I were starting my investments all over again today, would I really invest in the same old stocks I already have?

A basic assumption is that you want to maximize your returns for your level of risk. If we take the portfolio of all your assets, we must consider how they affect returns (and risk) when added together. We should in theory include your house, pension, your car and any antiques or furniture. But since you would be homeless without your house and penniless in old age without your pension, we shall ignore these. We are only considering your basic financial investments here.

Portfolio returns added together

An illustration of how and why returns on different shares go in different directions is shown in Table 5.3. You can see the profits during the year of an ice cream maker and an umbrella manufacturer. It is clear that if you held both you would be exposed to the good times all the year round.

Table 5.3   Ice cream maker/umbrella manufacturer and stock prices

	Ice cream maker		Umbrella manufacturer	
	Profits	Share price	Profits	Share price
Spring	100	20.0	500	40
Summer	800	30.0	100	30
Autumn	200	27.5	100	30
Winter	100	25.0	500	50

Portfolio risk added together

Your portfolio's risk changes markedly when rebalancing it between two basic asset classes – bonds and equities. If you have 100 per cent of your portfolio in equities, the risk will be high; if 100 per cent in bonds much less. If half and half, then you benefit from some exposure to equities at lower risk. This is not just a matter of simply weighting the risk. The key insight of Modern Portfolio Theory (MPT) is that risk of individual stocks bounce off each other in different ways when grouped together.[7]

> **One thing you should always be on the lookout to avoid
> is a group of stocks going down together.**

A portfolio that contains too many stable and mature companies is badly diversified. They will all go down together. A portfolio that contains too many companies that are expected to be the next Microsoft is also badly diversified. They too have a habit of losing the confidence of the market at the same time.

This less obvious point is that a portfolio of individually high risk assets may be less risky than a portfolio of low risk assets, providing the high risk stocks do not all move in tandem one with the other. In the language of Harry B. Markowitz, the founder of MPT, the riskiness of a portfolio depends on the 'covariance' of its holdings – how they interact – not on the average riskiness of the separate investments.

Choice is global

The choice of investment is a global one. There is no reason why returns should be higher in your home country than in other countries. You may decide that you want to try and invest in the best companies in the world. There is no reason why you should not. In a portfolio you can achieve greater diversification by investing in other countries and benefit from a wider selection of perhaps higher quality assets.

If you over-concentrate on your home country, you may be missing out on such opportunities. The downside risk is currency exposure. If your foreign assets go up but the currency depreciates you may lose out. A broadly diversified international portfolio should reduce overall risk and give you access to opportunities not available at home.

The New York Stock Exchange (NYSE), the largest stock exchange in the world, offers stock issued by over 3000 companies. On the NASDAQ, where technology stocks are traded informally, another 7000 stocks can be traded, many of them from companies operating outside the USA.

In London there are 2500 companies, a fifth of which are foreign. In Tokyo there are 1700 stocks. In France there are 660 and in Germany 355. The trend towards combining exchanges and computerized technologies means that the markets of the future will not be physically located anywhere – they will be global and fully automated.

How do the professionals manage money?

Fund management is big business. By the end of September 1999 collectively managed funds worldwide were worth over $9.4 trillion. A staggering 30,000 separate funds around the world fulfil demand. And demand shows no signs of falling off.

It is not unusual for a firm to be managing tens of thousands of millions. The largest firms, such as Schroders Investment Management, manage over £100bn. Many of the funds managed are pension funds and therefore tax free. They can be aggressively managed with no concerns about building up tax liabilities. The turnover of funds, the percentage of the fund bought and sold in a year, can often amount to 100 per cent. As fund managers have ballooned in size, so has their minimum unit of investment. A fund of £5000m with a well-diversified portfolio

> ..... Fund management is big business. .....

of a hundred stocks may have a minimum unit size 'building block' of £50m. Such size means that it is difficult for them to get in and out of stocks quickly and also means a whole raft of smaller companies are simply below the radar screen of fund managers. The results of this problem of size are hundreds of smaller companies that are under-researched and offer opportunities to private investors prepared to do the legwork.

Typically, a fund management house will be resourced with information from an in-house team of analysts and support from brokerages that they patronize. They will have a stream of management visitors from the companies in which they invest and they will go

> ..... We could not beat the market because we had become the market. .....

and see companies in which they have an interest. Their technology will include all manner of data feeds, risk optimizers and stock screening and monitoring software. Their performance will be audited by outside firms of investment consultants such as William Mercer or Frank Russell.

Fund managers themselves are typically recruited from the ranks of analysts, from accountancy or MBA programmes and from industry. They will probably have studied at good universities and may have additional qualifications such as the Chartered Financial Analyst (CFA) program or the associate exams of the UK Society of Investment Professionals (UKSIP).

One key difference in the management of portfolios by private and professional investors is in the assessment of risk. Private investors rely on intuition as a rough yardstick to measure their risk. Professional investors need to measure and quantify their risk. They want to see a concrete number that tells them how risky their portfolio is compared to the market and they have the computer resources (optimizers) to monitor this minute by minute if they wish. If the risk is unsatisfactory, they can rebalance their portfolios to a desired level.

Following on from the development of cheap computing power and the theory of efficient markets (EMH) is the development of indexation. If the market is assumed to be perfectly efficient, then what use are fund managers? You might as well just invest in the whole market portfolio rather than waste money trying to beat it. Fund managers don't like index funds on the whole, but they delight in the fact that transaction costs prevent index funds from matching indices. The reality is that different indices underperform each other.

The first such fund was put together by Wells Fargo in 1971 and invested in 1500 US stocks in an attempt to match the index. This it did tolerably well. Index funds have grown apace ever since, particularly in the USA. Index funds comprised $275bn dollars in 1995. In the UK the six largest tracker unit trusts amounted to £6bn at the time of writing (2001).

One typical large US index fund is the California Public Employee Retirement System (CALPERS), which invests 'over $20 billion dollars in stocks with one manager and two part-time traders. The traders sit in a room no bigger than a kitchen, surrounded by ten computer terminals with brightly coloured screens alive with jumping numbers'.[8] Let's hope nobody accidentally switches the electricity off.

Cutting the equities cake

Once you have decided how to divide your investments between cash, bonds and equities, your next challenge is how you cut your equities cake.

One strategy of traditional fund managers was to buy one stock big. When I arrived at my first fund management job, I was startled to find huge amounts of Racal and Vodafone in all the portfolios. It turns out that one fund manager used to just

> Your next challenge is how you cut your equities cake.

pick out stocks he liked and buy 5 or 10 per cent of them. One such was Racal Electronics. So when Racal spun off its mobile telecommunication division, the portfolios received a large chunk of Vodafone, which shortly became one of the world's largest telecom companies.[9]

This kind of approach – buying the best stocks in each industry paying little regard to weightings – can be successful, but also concentrates the risk of underperforming the index. It is an approach that is more appealing for a private investor who may be looking for 15 or 20 stocks rather than the 100 in a typical fund manager's portfolio. The private investor will be able to concentrate on a few stocks, whereas a professional will be forced to spread his or her attentions far and wide.

Sectors

Keeping up with the market means keeping up with its sectors. The most obvious way to avoid underperforming the index is to buy all the shares that make up the index, in other words, to match it exactly, forming a 'closet index fund'. This is easy for a large fund manager, although many forget to reduce their charges from those suitable for an expensively researched active fund to those justified by a passive index tracker. A more realistic approach would be to pick out the best stock(s) in every industry. If the latter is impracticable, you could select industries that are promising or dominate an index and pick out the best stocks among them.

> Keeping up with the market means keeping up with its sectors.

Don't forget that there is often a difference between an industry and the sectors that make up a stock market index and are decided by the index provider. Many investment professionals are contemptuous of the whole notion of arbitrary sectors determined by a public body which may not reflect the reality of an industry or suit the way fund managers invest.

Whichever technique you prefer, you need to take a view of sectors. There are two ways of forming a view of sectors. The first is the top-down approach, which uses macroeconomic factors to determine your bias towards a sector. The second is the bottom-up approach, which focuses on the health of the companies that make up the sectors. Since I am now going to have to dwell on a little economics, I would recommend anyone who finds economics intolerably dull simply to turn to the next chapter.

Top-down sector picking

To take a macroeconomic view of sectors, you need to track down various indicators of economic cycles. Leading indicators include factors that usually reach peaks or troughs ahead of the general economy. Lagging indicators normally trail the peaks and troughs of an economic cycle. Examples of leading indicators would be claims for unemployment and stock prices while a lagging indicator would be production of various heavy goods. There are several useful indicators published by the Office of National Statistics in the UK, the National Bureau of Economic Research (NBER) in the USA and Columbia University's CIBCR.

There are two types of basic economic changes. Cyclical changes arise when the business cycle moves from peak to trough and back again. Structural changes are more long term and reflect major change in the way the economy functions: for example, the transition of the eastern bloc countries from communist to capitalist and the emergence of new internet information distribution technologies.

Cyclical changes

It follows that different sectors are impacted by economic change in different ways. Investors can rotate their exposure to benefit from industry sectors in the different stages of the business cycle. The typical pattern would be that towards the end of a recession financial stocks excel as investors anticipate better times, rising bank earnings and demand for loans.

Once the economy begins to recover, businesses start thinking about modernizing their equipment and expanding services so capital goods industries such as machine tool manufacturers become attractive. Towards the peak of a business cycle, the rate of inflation increases. Basic raw materials therefore increase in price and their producers, such as oil, timber and steel, benefit. During a recession, consumer staples where demand is inflexible do best, so food, beverages and pharmaceuticals should outperform.

Clearly every economic cycle is different, but the above patterns make a lot of sense. Other sectors impacted by specific factors can be identified. High inflation will benefit raw material producers and property companies, but damage consumers of these products. High interest rates will benefit banks, but damage highly leveraged sectors such as construction, hotels, retail and ship owners. A high currency will benefit importers while damaging exporters.

Structural changes

Demographics are one big structural change. In the past 50 years the USA has had a baby boom, those born between the end of World War II and the early 1960s. This has had a large impact on US consumption and in areas such as housing, social security and health care. Other demographic changes around the world include ethnic mix, the geographical location of people and the distribution of income.

Government regulation can impact sectors. This applies particularly to the monopoly or quasi-monopoly industries such as gas and water supply or banks. Government also impacts on the

> Demographics are one big structural change.

pharmaceutical industry in approving new drugs and on financial services in providing consumer protection.

Another influence on sectors is lifestyle changes in how people live. This includes the increase in divorces and dwellings occupied by a single person along with changes in fashions, entertainment and working patterns.

Technology changes can affect any number of sectors in different ways. For example, bar code scanning allows retailers to manage their stocks better and increase their return on capital. Smaller planes can reduce the market share of railways. The internet can provide low cost distribution.

Computer screening

Rather than spend time looking at individual companies, many professional fund managers apply screens using computer databases. Screens narrow down the list of thousands of possible investments according to set criteria. An example would be stocks that have a low P/E, low Price/Book, high ROE or other attributes. Another use of computers is to determine companies with momentum or growth in earnings or share price. We will look at this in the next chapter.

Bottom-up stock picking

This entails taking a view on individual companies or a group of companies within an industry. We have already covered this in Step One. Essentially you apply your analysis to the individual companies and this drives the selection of which stocks to put into your portfolio. This is usually used alongside some input from the top-down approach, for instance on the economic environment of a company, but it is basically an exercise in stock picking.

Tactical timing

You may find that you have a choice on when to time your entry into the market. If you delay, you could lose out if the market is rising or gain if the market is falling since your block of cash will buy less or more shares. It is possible to use options on the index or individual stocks to get a rough match of exposure to the change in the index if required. Futures contracts offer a rather more precise exposure. Both instruments are used to get exposure to the market or to bet against it (go short of it). Fund managers would typically use futures prior to receiving a new block of funds to invest in order to protect themselves from underperformance. They may also use futures to gear exposure up or down if the market looks like shifting in one direction or another.

Recently many individual investors have taken to using derivatives to speculate, but this seems more likely to be a function of the desire of brokers to win commissions rather than any inherent advantage that private investors possess over professional investors.

NOTES

1   Charles Ellis and James Vertin, *The Investor's Anthology: Original Ideas from the Industry's Greatest Minds* (Wiley, New York, 1997), p. 161.

2   Charles Ellis and James Vertin, *The Investor's Anthology: Original Ideas from the Industry's Greatest Minds* (Wiley, New York, 1997), p. 90.

3   Issued by Credit Suisse First Boston (Europe) Ltd, Economics and Equity Research, *2001 Equity Gilt Study*, by Robert Barrie, Robert Jukes, Richard Kersley, Anna Mackman CFA, Steve Wright and William Porter, London, April 2001.

4   The optimal risk return trade off for each investor lies on the efficient frontier. The efficient frontier represents the set of portfolios (rather than individual securities) that has the maximum rate of return for every given level of risk. The optimal portfolio is the portfolio on the efficient frontier that has the highest utility for a given investor.

5   *The Collected Writings of John Maynard Keynes*, Donald Moggridge, ed., Vol XII. (Cambridge University Press, New York, 1983), p. 247.

6   Frank Reilly and Keith Brown, *Investment Analysis and Portfolio Management* (Harcourt Brace, London, 2000), p. 69.

7   To calculate the efficient frontier for a 1000 share universe for all possible portfolios using Markowitz's methodology requires no fewer than 499,500 calculations.

8   Peter Berstein, *Capital Ideas* (Free Press, New York, 1993), p. 193.

9   That fund manager was Tom O'Connell and when Guardian Asset Management was taken over by AXA Investment Managers, dominated by its AXA Rosenberg quantitative division, Tom took the opportunity to move on. He is now running funds at Ely Fund Management.

9

Doing your research

THE INFORMATION PROBLEM

When I chat to private investors, one of the most common things that comes across is that a majority think that choosing winning stocks does not require much effort. They are willing to risk their hard-earned cash on the back of some weakly researched tip or newspaper report. If it was that easy to make money on the stock market, then why should they tell you? If only they knew how shallow is the average journalist's knowledge of business. Under pressure of time reporters will uncritically rewrite copies of press releases knowing little of the business they are writing about.

Few private investors have read official sources such as the stock exchange filings because they are written in a style that puts off most readers. Nor do most people look at sectoral information or independent sources. Occasionally they may see a broker's report, but that event is a rarity. Television coverage is normally so simplified as to eradicate useful meaning. Even among provincial stockbrokers and City types, reliance on the media is considerable. Since the output of the news media, unlike the securities analysts, is unregulated, private investors are exposed to whatever bias the media choose to impose on the information. The lack of training and resources compounds the problem as stories go completely unchallenged. It is unusual for business reporters to have even a business degree or elementary work experience in commerce. Because of the lustre of respectability bestowed by a news article, many exaggerations, factual inaccuracies or omissions can slip through.

> A majority think that choosing winning stocks does not require much effort.

It is true that the effort of researching a security may seem to outweigh the benefits. But that is only because few private investors have been taken aside and properly instructed in how to do the research. Many do not distinguish between the primary sources containing fairly authoritative facts and the secondary sources that put a spin on them. So the object of this chapter is to get you up to speed on cutting through the information jungle.

PRIMARY SOURCES

The primary sources are relatively few and can now be easily obtained on the internet. For UK companies, the compulsory company filings with the stock exchange are available on the Regulatory News Service (RNS) and distributed for convenient display to sites such as Ample Interactive Investor and Hemmington Scott.

> The primary sources are relatively few and can now be easily obtained on the internet.

The annual and half-yearly (interim) reports will contain accurate updates about current market conditions and how the firm is faring. Other essential RNS announcements such as investments or acquisitions can also be easily found. Many annual reports can be ordered online or otherwise obtained by a quick phone call to the company secretary.

The other main corporate information you need in order to select a stock is some detail on the company's products and market share. While access to management would be ideal, this can now often be found in annual reports or on a corporate website where management presentations can be downloaded. General business conditions in the sectors can be found in accessible industry websites and magazines.

SECONDARY SOURCES

Digests of financial information (sales, profits, net assets, etc.) are available in the fundamental data areas of most of the big umbrella sites, although they can be difficult to find. Hemmington Scott (www.Hemscott.net) and Hoovers Online (www.hoovers.co.uk) specialize in presenting this fundamental information in an easy-to-use format. You will often find that the useful ratios such as P/E and Price/Book are readily available along with a summary of the business, financial statistics going back a couple of years and some details of shareholders and management. For US stocks the equivalent sites are Value Line and Standard & Poor's Stock Reports, which provide comprehensive information in an abbreviated format.

For more specific help in distinguishing the wheat from the chaff, there are magazines and tip sheets, broker reports and specialist websites. Tip sheets and magazines tend just to rewrite the basic facts and then add a rather intuitive 'buy' or 'sell' lacking any factual basis. The best investment magazines are *Investors Chronicle*, *Business Week* and *Forbes*. These have recently been joined by *Investors Week* and *Shares* magazines. All offer brief company-specific and sector articles, often derived from interviews with the brokers and analysts. Unfortunately the articles tend to shed a lot of the meaning in an effort to simplify complex situations.

Tip sheets have a generally mixed record, with tracking studies showing that picking stocks at random is a better bet. Therefore tip sheets are unable to charge heavily for their services and cannot afford appropriately qualified staff to

> .... With an Infinite number of Monkeys, some are bound to come up trumps. ....

research stocks properly. Ordinary private investors and bulletin boarders have contrasting views about tipsters. Referring to the common scatter-gun strategy of tipsters, Bri Blackdog comments: 'With an Infinite number of Monkeys, some are bound to come up trumps.' Matt Blacker is more of a spectator than a player using tipsters as a mere starting point: 'We need an initial source of info about shares and tipsters are as good a way as any of bringing a share into the spotlight. This should obviously be followed up by doing your own research (DYOR) and price monitoring before buying.'

Stan Kaiser values the shortcuts some tipsters claim to offer: 'In the end time, chance, contrary advice and every other variable makes you rely upon common sense and experience. But proven, inexpensive and quick advice is always worth it if you can get it. That is also how you run a business.' Jamie on Ample Interactive Investor's board is sceptical of any share being tipped: 'The danger is that it's only being ramped and that you might be sitting on a paper loss for some time.' John Slade points to the prevalence of tipsters during the technology stock boom: 'During the bull run in the market a child of twelve could have picked a string of winners. Since then they have lived off those good times. However, the tide has turned and they are now shown up as the charlatans they are. Let this be a lesson to us all.'

Of course there are alternative shortcuts for private investors. Specialist websites have now sprung up offering the expertise of highly qualified analysts to subscribers. These have the advantage of being independent of any corporate influences that may persuade a brokerage analyst to withhold a sell recommendation.

I must confess that I am a fan of the research reports of securities analysts. They contain basic information and forecasts along with a well-reasoned conclusion on whether to buy or sell the stock. The reader should be aware of potential conflicts of interest with the securities house sponsoring the reports. First, the company being researched may be a client. Second, the objective of the report may be to generate commission or help the firm's market makers. Analysts are also remarkably unwilling to stand out from their peers in forecasts. But as collections of important details, reports are unrivalled.

> I am a fan of the research reports of securities analysts.

HOW TO DO RESEARCH

Figure 9.1 illustrates how to go about industry research and company research.

Figure 9.1   Choosing sectors and picking stocks

RESEARCH CASE STUDY 1: THE HOUSEBUILDING INDUSTRY

This research case study illustrates how to use easily accessible information to do a DIY industry analysis. Once we have found an industry we like, we can then move on to the second stage of selecting some shares within it that look promising. Let's start by working through an example of how to get information to build up a view of the prospects for one part of a chosen industry, i.e. the housebuilding sector.

First, you have to work out what information you actually need to find. What are the questions you need to ask? With residential housing you need to work out the supply and demand for the end product (new houses.) You need to check the trends in the pricing and cost environment to consider the kind of factors that affect the profitability of the companies involved in housebuilding.

What is the demand for houses and market activity?

For housebuilding the obvious key statistic of the health of the industry is house prices. I consulted the house price and affordability surveys on the Halifax Group (www.halifaxgroupplc.co.uk) and Nationwide (www.nationwide.co.uk) websites, along with government statistics (www.statistics.gov.uk) on the number of dwellings, population statistics showing the number of households and statistics showing housing market prices and mortgage completions. I then looked on the Nationwide and Bank of England (www.bankofengland.co.uk) websites for details of the trends in consumer lending. After doing that I looked at the Inland Revenue (www.inlandrevenue.gov.uk) statistics which show government revenues from Stamp Duty.

What is the supply of houses? For supply of houses I again consulted government statistics (www.statistics.gov.uk) for the number of completions and starts and then compared them to the more recent data from NHBC (www.nhbc.co.uk) which is the main insurer of building works in the UK and can tell us how many homes have been registered with it recently.

What are the cost trends in housebuilding? To determine housebuilding cost trends I examined the website of the government body that monitors building costs, the Building Costs Information Service (www.bcis.co.uk), and copied their graph. For trends in the costs of land, I consulted a firm of surveyors, Savills (www.fpdsavills.co.uk), and examined their graph showing the costs of residential building land.

Here are the results of an afternoon's work churning the housebuilding industry information on these websites:

Step 1: Demand and supply

Statistic 1: Housing stock by type

Conclusion from evidence: demographic information shows that demand for owner-occupied dwellings has been increasing at a slowing rate and may now be hitting a ceiling (Table 9.1).

Table 9.1 Demand and supply of housing

Stock type	1938	March 1979	March 2000 (provisional)
All tenures: number of dwellings	10.6m	17.6m	21.0m
Owner occupied	32%	56%	68%
Privately rented	57%	13%	12%
Local authority rented	11%	29%	14%
Registered social landlord (RSL) rented	N/a	2%	6%

Source: http://www.housing.dtlr.gov.uk/research/hss/hs2000/index.htm#1

Statistic 2: Household numbers

Conclusion from evidence: population information shows the number of households increasing with a forecast rate of 152,000 new dwellings per year. This number excludes the replacement demand that will be required when houses fall down, fall into the sea, etc. (Table 9.2).

Table 9.2 Household numbers

Households	1996	1999	2021 (estimated)	Change 1996-2021
Total number of households	20.2m	20.7m	24.0m	+3.8m
One-person households	5.8m	6.1m	8.5m	+2.7m
Average household size (persons)	2.40	2.36	2.15	-0.25

Source: http://www.housing.dtlr.gov.uk/information/keyfigures/index.htm

Statistic 3: New housebuilding

Conclusion from evidence: on the supply and demand front, supply of houses remains fairly weak at 137,000 completions last year, compared to 155,000 in 1991. But builders started work on 144,000 houses, compared to 134,000 in 1991 (Table 9.3).

Table 9.3   New housebuilding

	1991 Starts	1991 Completions	2000 Starts	2000 Completions
Private enterprise	114,000	131,000	131,000	120,000
Registered social Landlords (RSL)	16,000	15,000	13,000	18,000
Local authorities	3,000	8,000	200	500
Total	134,000	155,000	144,000	137,000

Source: http://www.housing.dtlr.gov.uk/information/keyfigures/index.htm

Statistic 4: NHBC data new build registrations and completions

Conclusion from evidence: 90 per cent of new homes are insured with NHBC with whom they register at start and finish of the new build. So we can track the trends on new homes registered and completed in the UK. In May 2001 registrations show a 6 per cent increase on May 2000. There are more registrations than completions. Completions fell by 5 per cent over the last year. This is slightly more up to date than the numbers available from the government which show that in the year 2000 completions were less than starts (Tables 9.4 and 9.5).

Table 9.4   New build registrations, all sectors

Year	Jan	Feb	Mar	Apr	May	Year to date
2000	13,044	14,021	16,363	11,670	12,673	67,771
2001	14,526	11,846	13,521	11,511	13,398	64,802
	+11%	−16%	−17%	−1%	+6%	−4%

Source: www.nhbc.co.uk

Table 9.5 New build completions, all sectors

Year	Jan	Feb	Mar	Apr	May	Year to date
2000	11,886	11,487	13,278	11,909	13,541	62,101
2001	11,447	9,806	12,379	11,792	12,887	58,311
	–4%	–15%	–7%	–1%	–5%	–6%

Source: www.nhbc.co.uk

Step 2: What's going on with house prices and affordability?

Statistic 5: Halifax house price index

Conclusion from evidence: prices are rising above the average long-term rate (Table 9.6). According to the Nationwide: 'The long-run trend in annual house price growth is around 5–6 per cent in London compared to 4–5 per cent in the UK as a whole.' The City and the large number of company headquarters in London create an unusual market (Figures 9.3, 9.4, 9.5).

Table 9.6 Halifax house price index

Halifax house price index		Monthly change	Annual change	Average house price
1983	100			£30,898
June 2001	298.2	1.6%	9.7%	£92,122

Source: http://www.halifaxgroupplc.co.uk/view/housepriceindex/hpi_historic_data.xls

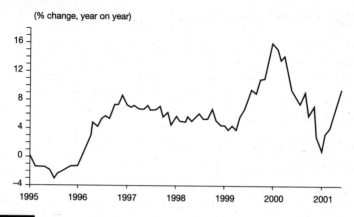

Figure 9.2 The Halifax publishes the annual rate of house price inflation on its website

Source: http://www.halifaxgroupplc.co.uk/view/economicview.asp

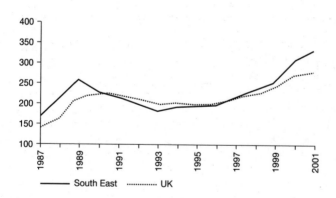

Figure 9.3 Halifax house price index, South East – Quarter 1, 2001

Source: http://www.halifaxgroupplc.com/view/housepriceindex/press/images/south_east_2.gif

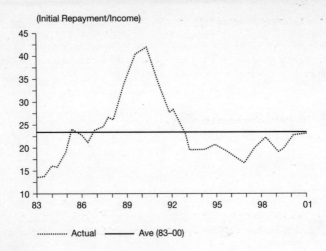

Figure 9.4   **Housing affordability, South East**

Source: http://www.halifaxgroupplc.com/view/housepriceindex/press/london.asp

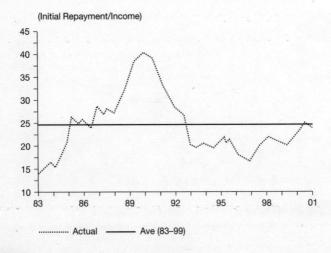

Figure 9.5   **Housing affordability, Greater London**

Source: http://www.halifaxgroupplc.com/view/housepriceindex/press/london.asp

Statistic 6: Private housing market statistics

Conclusion from evidence: the statistics show prices rising and first time buyers dropping out. In 1979 they were 45 per cent of completions. In 2000 they were 42 per cent of completions (Table 9.7).

Table 9.7   Private housing market statistics

	1979	2000 Quarter 1	2001 Quarter 1	% Change 2000–01
Average house price: England	£20,000	£102,000	£113,000	+11.1%
Mortgage completions (UK)	715,000	218,000	204,000	−6.4%
Of which first time buyers	323,000	102,000	86,000	−16.0%
Average mortgage rate (UK) at end of period	11.9%	7.06%	6.73%	N/a

Source: http://www.housing.dtlr.gov.uk/information/keyfigures/index.htm

Step 3: Underlying market activity

Statistics 7 and 8: Government and Bank of England lending data

Conclusion from evidence: lending is at an historic high while savings are at lows. Recently Bank of England statistics show that lending growth has tailed off (Figures 9.6, 9.7).

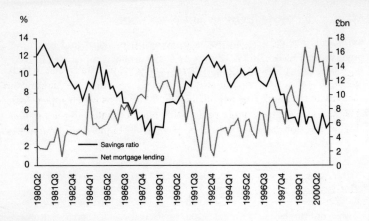

Figure 9.6   **Mortgage lending and savings ratio**
Source: Nationwide, ONS

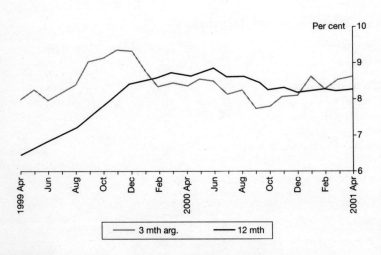

Figure 9.7   **Growth rates of seasonally adjusted lending secured on dwellings**
Source: http://www.bankofengland.co.uk/mfsd/li/010531/sadw.jpg and
http://www.bankofengland.co.uk/mfsd/li/010531/lendindi.xls

Step 4: Geographical market activity

Statistic 9: Inland Revenue regional Stamp Duty

Conclusion from evidence: by using the Inland Revenue data on Stamp Duty payable each time a property transacts, we can see significant activity in the South East of England over other areas which appear to be stagnant. Of course a large part of this will be related to the fact that higher rates of Stamp Duty will be payable on higher value properties (Table 9.8).

Table 9.8   Inland Revenue regional Stamp Duty

	1996–7	1997–8	1998–9
England and Wales	625	800	1,015
North East	10	15	15
North West	45	50	60
Yorkshire and Humberside	30	35	40
Midlands	30	35	40
West Midlands	45	50	60
East	70	90	110
London	165	235	320
South East	150	200	255
South West	65	80	95
Wales	15	20	20
UK	675	875	1,110

Source: http://www.inlandrevenue.gov.uk/stats/table15_3.htm

Step 5: The industry cost base

Statistic 10: Building costs index

Conclusion from evidence: costs are rising only slowly and present no immediate threat to the industry (Figure 9.8).

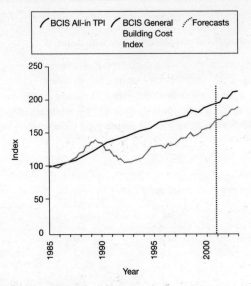

Figure 9.8	**Building and tender price trends**

Source: www.bcis.co.uk. With kind permission of BCIS Limited

Statistic 11: Land prices

Conclusion from the evidence: year-on-year growth in land prices and house prices corresponds with land prices rising and falling at a far faster rate. The recent fall in land prices indicates that house prices may follow (Figure 9.9).

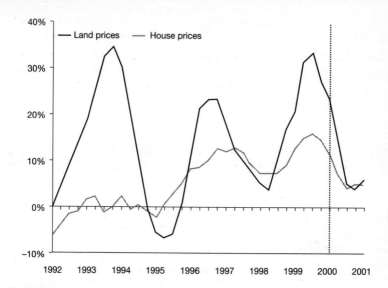

Figure 9.9 **Land prices and house prices**

Source: www.fpdsavills.co.uk. With permission of FPD Savills Residential Research Department

Decision time

The statistics show a sector with strong fundamental characteristics of demand and supply. It is at a mature stage in its recovery from the lows reached in the early to mid-1990s. Short-term signals are that the market has run ahead of prices that are acceptable in the London region, but elsewhere the picture looks fairly stable. Costs appear to be stable. The key growth area is currently the South East with the likelihood that prices in other regions may catch up. We shall now look at a housebuilder in more detail.

RESEARCH CASE STUDY 2:
THE BERKELEY GROUP PLC

What are the alternative companies in the sector? If we look in the share price pages of the *Financial Times* we find that there are 14 or so house-builders, including names we are all familiar with such as Barratts, Wimpey and McAlpine. However, because of the evidence in our case study we decide to focus on the South East so we consult the property supplements of national newspapers and look for a company that is advertising heavily in the South East. Berkeley Homes fits the bill. It is focused on high-value homes in London and the South East.

What is the company's key product?

The company's product is obviously new houses. But what type and where? We consult the company's website www.berkeleygroup.co.uk. For The Berkeley Group plc the key product appears to be premium, high-value homes in London and the South East of England.

We next look at the investor relations section of the company's website which contains news releases for the last two final and interim results. We ring up the company secretary and ask for a copy of the annual report. In the meantime we download the most recent results from both the website and the RNS filings on the Ample Interactive Investor website. In the Results statement we find the Chairman's comments and detailed financial results, all of which we download. There are lots of useful nuggets of information, including the fact that the company's average selling price is £251,000 with 2915 units sold in 2000.

Is it growing?

To answer this question we need to consult the basic facts. We could use the annual reports or a service such as Hemmington Scott's REFS. But since the company website conveniently contains all the information we need, we shall use that. We can see the record from the company's investor relations site and annual reports. In the last year profits are up 24 per cent. They show three-year earnings per share growth of 62.6 per cent or 17.6 per cent pa.

From the results statement on the website, the actual number of units sold in 2001 appears to be falling. However, this is because of the company's strategy of focusing on higher value units at higher margins. The same results show the average unit price in 2001 has risen to £278,000 from £251,000. This much is stale news. What we want to know is whether Berkeley can keep up the pace (Table 9.9).

Table 9.9 The Berkeley Group plc growth

The Berkeley Group plc	1996	1997	1998	1999	2000
Turnover/sales (m)	334.3	485.3	599.6	697.3	798.9
Profit before tax (m)	43.4	75.1	100.3	110.4	143.6
Earnings per share (p)	33.3	49.3	60.6	62.9	80.2
Dividend (p)	8.0	9.1	10.3	11.2	12.9

Source: www.berkeleygroup.co.uk. With permission of The Berkeley Group plc

We next look at the consensus earnings estimates in Ample Interactive Investor's quote for Berkeley stock. This is under the Broker Forecasts tab. We find that earnings growth of 9 per cent is forecast. Then we turn to the Chairman's statement to determine how things look from his perspective. Apparently all is going well:

> The housing market in the past 12 months has been very solid … Early in 2001 there were some concerns about the impact on the housing market of the 'dot com' shake-out and the falls in the stock market. Any such effect was offset by falling interest rates, however, and the market has remained healthy for the first half of 2001.

> Many factors interact to determine the buoyancy of the housing market and one of these is the house price/earnings ratio which, in London and the South East, is relatively high. Equally, interest rates are low, which makes homes more affordable, while employment is high. The feel-good factor, so important to the confidence of our purchasers, continues to be strong. Sales reservations in May and to this point in June have been at record levels.

The Chairman goes on to comment on the current level of sales:

> The year has started strongly with the level of sales reservations ahead of previous years and also at excellent margins. We now have a number of very large schemes under construction and these will make meaningful contributions in the current year. We believe that the Group is excellently

placed to make further progress in the medium term. As long as the housing market remains satisfactory, we look forward with confidence to another successful year in 2001/2002.

Can it sustain growth?

The key factors for sustaining growth in a housebuilder are obviously the availability of land on which to build and capital to sustain growth. According to the Chairman's statement the company now controls 19,400 plots of land, which represent around seven years of supply: i.e. 19,400 divided by this year's units sold of 2915. Again in the Chairman's statement it was revealed that planning was obtained on 7000 plots in 2000 alone. So there seems no problem on that front.

What about costs? How do the company's financial numbers and ratios shape up? We again look at the accounts. The margin (PBT divided by turnover) has risen from 15.8 per cent in 1999 to 17.9 per cent in 2000 and is flirting with 20 per cent in the interim results. The gearing (long-term debt divided by net assets) is modest at around 28 per cent with interest cover very high. In the financial year ending 30 April 2000, the return on equity (net profits/shareholders equity) was 13.4 per cent against 11.8 per cent last year.

What is its market position?

According to Chairman's statement downloaded from the website:

> During the past five years, we have placed increasing emphasis on urban regeneration and have built up the skills and expertise to undertake the more difficult and complicated schemes which this involves. With the Group's commitment to sustainability, such schemes, we believe, will be the thrust of our development in the future and reinforce Berkeley's status as one the country's leading urban regenerators.

We go to the broker research website Multex Investor (www.multexinvestor.co.uk) and consult an analyst's report, 'Berkeley Group, strongly positioned in a healthy market', by Clyde Lewis of HSBC. We find that The Berkeley Group is viewed by the analyst as a market leader in urban developments, particularly in the South East.

There are two free recent broker reports, one by Merrill Lynch and the other by HSBC on the Multex website. The HSBC report is a *buy* recommendation. It reveals that earnings growth of 18 per cent is forecast for the next year. According to the HSBC analyst: 'We continue to see Berkeley as a well-positioned stock in a cheap subsector. Its long land bank and focus on inner city, mixed use schemes should ensure its growth rate exceeds the sector in the medium term.' There is some useful detail in the report on the historical margin trends and the long run average selling price. A useful piece of information contained in the HSBC report is that, by type of property built, apartments now account for 70 per cent of completions. A full accounts spreadsheet gives a detailed breakdown of where the profits are coming from.

A different view is contained in Merrill Lynch's update, where they rate the company a 'long term neutral'. Earnings growth of 13.8 per cent is forecast for the coming year: 'Forward sales at secure high margins and the breadth of revenue sources including unlocked commercial property profits, underpins 10 per cent plus growth in the next 2 years.'

Different reports have different styles. The Merrill Lynch report comes with a complicated rating system that it is probably safe to ignore. There are rafts of complicated numbers including EV/EBITDA, EV/Sales. EV stands for enterprise value. But most of the numbers can be easily translated. For instance, Price/Book is the price divided by the book value and is 1.09, indicating the price is close to the book assets. CFPS is cash flow per share and for Berkeley it is £1 per share. This is clearly a very cash generative business at the moment, well supported by asset value.

The HSBC report is much more enthusiastic and points to the recent sales records in May and June along with the fact that the company has strengthened its land bank in the past 12 months to secure future sites.

Both reports stress the modest P/E ratio relative to the entire sector. Berkeley is trading on a P/E of 7.2x 2001 earnings whereas the sector as a whole is said to trade on 7x 2001 earnings. Merrills has a useful number indicating that the 2002 P/E is 40 per cent of the home market 2002 P/E. Since the 2002 P/E for Berkeley is stated at 6.7x the whole market must be trading at 16.75×2002 earnings. Either way the company is trading at a huge discount.

Management quality

We look on the website and see a list of impressive biographies of non-executive and some long-serving internal candidates, including the co-founder of the company, Anthony Pidgely, who is Group Managing

Director. We check the latest news announcements to the stock exchange whereby companies must reveal any director changes. These are listed in the 'News' tab in the price quotation for The Berkeley Group on the Ample Interactive Investor website.

We find that the founder's son (Tony K. Pidgely) is leaving the company. The annual report contains details of director shareholdings and reveals that collectively they own 5.395 million and have options over 3.3 million shares. There is comfort for the City in having Fred Wellings, who wrote the book on how to analyze the sector, on the board as a non-executive director. According to Merrill Lynch: 'If visibility, deliverability and sustainability are the golden rules of success then Berkeley certainly scores 2 out of 3.'

Are the pros buying?

We again check the 'News' tab in the Berkeley quote on the Ample Interactive Investor website for stock exchange announcements. There has been a flurry of buy and sell deals around the end of the US tax year by the founder, A.W. Pidgely, alongside the exercise of an option. Since they seem to net out at little change we shall assume that they are tax related.

Among the institutions, Aegon and Fidelity have been selling a little on recent weakness while Morgan Stanley and Legal and General have been buying. All retain significant stakes with Morgan Stanley taking advantage of weakness to buy a 3 per cent stake from a zero position.

Is the share price reasonable?

We conclude that it is:

- P/E for the coming year is at a discount to the sector while the exposure to growth areas indicates it has a higher quality exposure to the sector's underlying favourable prospects.
- Growth seems assured by favourable market conditions and a long pipeline of sites on which to build.
- Company finances are strong enough to support growth and conservative enough to withstand a downturn.

Risks?

1. The HSBC broker report highlights the following risks. The house-building sector has traditionally boomed when interest rates were falling and bust when they were rising. With rates turning up, there is a risk of bust. However interest rates are not likely to rise as much as in past cycles and so the risk may be overstated. The biggest risk is of a full-scale economic downturn that hits confidence. But this is not currently a strong likelihood.

2. The Merrill Lynch report highlights the same risks, pointing out that exposure to rising interest rates is less than in previous cycles because of the higher prevalence of fixed interest rate mortgages. But it argues out that '70 per cent of new mortgages last year were fixed rate, for terms of up to five years'. In 1989 some 64 per cent of net earnings of a first-time buyer went on mortgage repayments; now the figure is 35 per cent. In London the corresponding figure was 74 per cent in 1989 and is 44 per cent now. So the exposure to changing interest rates is less pronounced than in previous cycles.

10

Online resources survey

Financial news

Newswires

UK data and market prices

Online resources have expanded at such a pace that they may appear to be overwhelming. It has never been truer that you have to look hard to find what you need and rigorously pick out material of quality and utility. So this guide has broken down the most useful sites to tune into the way you actually need to use them as tools to find the necessary facts in order to make profitable investments.

SELECTING STOCKS

Fundamentals

www.wilink.com   Offers free annual reports on thousands of companies in dozens of countries, not just the UK. Increasingly you can download them in a PDF file rather than getting them by post.

www.hemscott.net   Strong on basic accounts, director and advisor details and institutional shareholders. You have to subscribe to get many of the details.

www.hoovers.com/uk   Well-processed arrangements of financial data and useful links.

www.ir-soc.org.uk   The Investors Relations Society maintains a list of links to hundreds of investor relations sites maintained by the companies themselves. Companies' investor relations sites vary sharply in their usefulness, but are always worth checking.

BROKER RESEARCH REPORTS

www.multexinvestor.co.uk   The only site offering a comprehensive selection of broker research to the investing public. It stocks tens of thousands of reports on over 2500 companies and from 50 research providers. Also stocks international companies.

www.mlhsbc.com   Free summary research from the analysts of both Merrill Lynch and HSBC for account holders.

UK BROKER RANKINGS

www.tempestdirect.co.uk   Publishes an annual survey of the analysts as the Reuters Survey of UK larger and smaller companies. Also covers other geographical areas.

www.primarkextelsurvey.com   Primark Extel publishes a rival survey of much the same thing.

INDEPENDENT ANALYSIS

www.equityinvestigator.com   This excellent site offers specialized technology research from an entirely independent perspective by top-ranked former brokerage analysts, Anne McIvor and Judith Allen.

www.moneyguru.com   This subscription site offers company-by-company analysis and model portfolios.

www.breakingviews.com   Set up by Hugo Young, an FT journalist, this subscription site writes in the style of the *Financial Times* LEX column.

OTHER RESEARCH SITES

www.equity-development.co.uk   Focuses on smaller companies on the main market.

www.equitygrowth.net   Set up by former City analyst, Gareth Evans, this focuses on smaller and OFEX quoted companies.

www.unquoted.co.uk   This site focuses on OFEX companies.

www.itruffle.com   This site focuses on smaller companies in the main market and offers some company interviews and investor presentations for free.

STOCK SCREENING TOOLS

www.hemscott.net   Hemmington Scott's REFS is to my knowledge the most comprehensive screening tool available in the UK market and is modelled on those available to professional investors. At over £700pa it does not come cheap.

www.bridgefinancialsystems.com   This is the institutional version of Hemmington Scott's stock screens, although a version is available for retail customers.

www.stockscreener.com   This American site has free screens for US stocks.

www.stocksearch.com   Another American site with free screens on US stocks.

www.zachs.com   Has a number of limited screening tools.

www.thescreener.com   A subscription site that has a global screener which pulls out stocks using a mixture of technical and fundamental analysis. Some bits are available free on Yahoo Finance.

HELPFUL BROKER AND FUND MANAGER SITES

www.beesonresearch.co.uk   Beeson Gregory, a specialist investment bank, currently makes available all its research for users of its site who register for free.

www.charles-stanley.co.uk   Has a research section that offers some useful economic and sector weight information as well as stock screens on yield, Price/Book and PEG.

www.collins-stewart.co.uk   Offers smaller company research from its team of analysts and a technical analysis product from Chris Chaitow, a well-known technical analyst.

www.durlacher.co.uk   Durlacher, a technology and internet specialist, offers research and sector reports on its site.

www.redmayne.co.uk   Includes stock picks and daily market comment from Redmayne Bentley, a national chain of retail brokers.

www.mlhsbc.com   Free summary research from the analysts of both Merrill Lynch and HSBC for customers.

www.baring-asset.com   If you go into their private clients section, you can find updated news and views on the bond and equities markets from their research teams.

www.deam-uk.com   If you go into the institutional section you can find
their excellent market focus outlining Deutsche Asset Management's
views on the equities and bond markets.

www.chasefleming.com   In the asset management area you can find weekly
updated news and views from Chase Fleming's strategy department.

IPOs

www.nothingventured.com   Backed by Durlacher, the specialist technology
brokerage, this offers access to IPOs with a brokerage facility.

www.eo.com   A site with a European angle allowing you to apply for IPOs
online for a wider than usual range of issues.

www.issuesdirect.co.uk   Another site with a facility for applying for IPOs.

www.ipo.com   A big US site with the same aims as its UK equivalents and
a team of journalists covering the market.

ECONOMIC ANGLE

For fans of both the top-down and bottom-up approach to stock selection,
economists are always worth consulting. There is solid economic coverage on the sites of Chase Fleming, Deutsche Asset Management and Bar-
ing Asset Management. Best official sources for the UK are the Bank of
England and HM Treasury. For US economic information, the best source
is the Federal Reserve Bulletin, which is the monthly digest of the board of
governors of the Federal Reserve System. The Economic Intelligence Unit
(EIU) publishes reports on 160 countries, while *The Economist* looks at 100
countries. The United Nations publishes useful information for most UN
countries.

www.economist.com   A subscription site offering the contents of the weekly magazine and some useful archives and international data.

www.hm-treasury.gov.uk   A compact and well-designed government website with access to economic forecasts and indicators, budget details and
statistics such as the National Asset Register.

www.bog.frb.fed.us   Site of the US Federal Reserve System which has
detailed coverage of the US economy including the monthly bulletin.

www.chasefleming.com   Contains updated information on markets and strategy.

www.dam.com   Has some very high quality downloadable quarterly research from the company's strategy and research departments.

www.bankofengland.co.uk   The Bank of England Quarterly allows you to follow events in the economy and financial markets in as much detail as you can take. Good summaries on page one.

www.lombard-st.co.uk   Forecasts and coverage from Prof. Tim Congdon, a monetarist economist and former government advisor.

OFFICIAL RESOURCES

UK

www.companies-house.com   The main source for compulsory filing of accounts and information relating to all partnerships and companies in the UK. Useful for researching directorships. If you are interested in investigating whether that obscure company listed in the accounts really owns vast property assets or a hidden stake in the next Microsoft, this is the place to find out.

www.statistics.gov.uk   The main government website for UK statistics. Includes a cumbersome three-level database arranged by themes. The numbers you want are probably there if you look hard enough.

www.hm-treasury.gov.uk   The Treasury site contains access to lots of aggregate numbers such as the GDP and money supply numbers.

www.londonstockexchange.com   The official LSE site contains a useful database of statistics about sectors and individual stocks. It also has lots of detail on indices and listing procedures and rules.

www.open-gov.uk   This is the gateway to all the main UK government sites.

www.ofex.co.uk   The site is maintained by brokers JP Jenkins to display the prices at which they believe you can trade stocks that are members of the UK off-exchange facility (OFEX). OFEX is part of JP Jenkins.

Non-UK

www.easdaq.com   The site of the European version of the NASDAQ over-the-counter market for high technology exchange offers prices and information on all EASDAQ stocks.

www.europa.eu.int   The site for the European Union has access to plenty of statistics.

www.nasdaq.com   An exceptional website offering stock selection aids as well as pricing and information. It was one of the first sites with streaming self-updating information and is now offering a very good free stock screen.

www.nyse.com   The website of the largest stock exchange in the world. Contains (cumbersome) pricing information and some educational material.

www.edgar-online.com   One of the best examples of the use of the internet to my knowledge, although poorly designed. All US companies have to file their stock exchange documents here. Particularly useful once you work out what the document codes stand for, i.e. the 10K are the full year annual reports, the 9K is the interim unaudited half yearly report, while the 8K is filed each month and shows any change which affects debt or equity capital in issue.

TECHNICAL ANALYSIS

www.bigcharts.com   Has free charting on 24,000 securities and some free features such as 52-week highs and lows, momentum, stocks being shorted and other interesting indicators.

www.sta-uk.org   UK professional body of technical analysts.

www.mta.org   World professional body of technical analysts.

www.mta-usa.org   US branch of the world body of technical analysts.

www.trend-analysis.co.uk   UK subscription site for charting ideas.

www.traders.com   A US site with lots of trading ideas on US stocks.

www.elliotwaves.com   A site devoted to the Elliot Waves technique of technical analysis.

www.bollingerbands.com   One of a group of sites devoted to the theories of John Bollinger.

SECTORAL RESEARCH RESOURCES

Most of the major accountancy firms (Coopers, KPMG, etc.) provide sectoral reports on trends within the sectors, while several companies produce product and markets research.

www.ey.com/uk   Ernst & Young produces regular surveys by its in-house experts on the state of the UK corporate world, often providing useful sectoral views from a bean counter's vantage point.

www.mintel.com   Lots of regularly updated consumer reports.

www.datamonitor.com   A flow of large, well-researched reports with good graphs and predictions.

PHARMACEUTICALS AND BIOTECHNOLOGY

www.biochemsoc.org.uk   The Biochemical Society of the UK.

www.fda.org   The website of the Federal Drugs Administration which must approve all new drugs. Approvals are published on the website.

www.sturzas.com   Provides specialist biomedical research to subscribers.

www.newscientist.com   *New Scientist* is a popular weekly scientific magazine that provides easily understandable explanations of current issues and discoveries.

PROPERTY

www.estatesgazette.co.uk   This is the site of the property industry weekly, *Estates Gazette*, and includes plenty of information and links.

www.propertymall.co.uk   Propertymall includes links to sites of the large firms of surveyors. These often contain downloadable research and information of high quality.

www.rics.org   This site of the property industry professional body contains some useful price indices and information about the profession.

www.fpdsavills.co.uk   Like many of the sites of large professional firms of surveyors, Savills's website includes some of the output of its research department on market conditions.

www.weatheralls.co.uk   Produces some useful research on the state of the market.

MEDIA

www.nma.co.uk   Provides weekly news and comment on the media, internet, advertising and marketing worlds.

www.abc.org.uk   The Audit Bureau of Circulation carries a wealth of information on sales trends for the printed media.

CHEMICALS, INDUSTRIALS AND OILS

www.chemweek.com   *Chemicals Week* is the weekly magazine of the chemicals industry.

www.manufacturing.net   An umbrella for the global manufacturing industry with lots of useful links.

www.cia.org.uk   The site of the Chemical Industries Association has a range of industry information.

www.oilandgas.com   An umbrella site with links to many useful industry sites.

www.eia.doe.gov   The UK government department site (Environment) has lots of useful industry information.

www.miningnews.net   An excellent subscription site for researching resources stocks employing a team of award winning journalists and analysts. There are sections for gold, coal, nickel, diamonds and other resources with regular reports on sectors of interest.

BANKS AND FINANCIAL SERVICES

www.americanbanker.com   Site of the *American Banker*, an American banking magazine.

www.bsa.org.uk   The Building Society Association has useful information on lending and the state of the housing market.

www.fsa.gov.uk   The site of the UK's super-regulatory body for financial services.

TECHNOLOGY

www.siliconinvestor.com   A leading US site focused on technology stocks providing market news, analysis and discussion boards. Parts of the site are for subscribers only.

www.redherring.com   Red Herring is a breaking news and information site for the technology industry with a US focus. Parts of the site are subscription only.

SELECTING OTHER ASSETS

Fixed interest securities (bonds)

The kind of information required to pick a bond is of course very different from equities. There is less emphasis on fundamental analysis. Bond investors need information on:

- the direction of interest rates
- the inflation rates
- the features of the bonds.

Some of this information is available in the economic sources listed above but there is also specialist information available from the leading credit rating agencies, Standard & Poor's, Moodys and Fitch. Information on bond prices can usually be found in the *Financial Times* or on Bloomberg.

www.bloomberg.co.uk   Has a number of sections covering the bonds market and interest rates.

www.psa.com   The site of the US Public Securities Association shows how far ahead the USA is in popularizing bond investing.

www.bondsonline.com   A comprehensive site for the US-oriented bond investor with news and commentary, tools and calculators. Has useful sections on the various categories of US bonds, along with coverage of yield spreads for US corporate bonds. There is even a chat room.

www.fitchibca.com   The site of rating agency Fitch IBCA contains news of changes in ratings.

Venture Capital

www.bvca.co.uk   Website of the British Venture Capital Association. Useful to both entrepreneurs and investors.

www.3igroup.com   3i Group is one of the largest UK venture capital funds. Useful for finding out what the professionals are investing in right now.

www.jpmhq.com   Hambrech and Quist are a large international technology-oriented fund. Again useful to know where the professionals are directing their investments.

www.venturedome.com   A news site aimed at professionals in the venture capital industry with good stories on the latest industry events.

Hedge funds

www.hedgefund.net   HedgeFund.net is a listing of hedge fund information and performance that currently encompasses 31 different strategies. It includes over 1800 of the world's most talented hedge fund managers.

www.tassresearch.com   This database of some 2000 hedge fund providers collects information on the types of strategies followed, along with details of the managers.

Alternative assets

www.trend-analysis.co.uk   This site is focused on foreign exchange and commodities research.

www.assetalt.com   A US-focused site looking at alternative assets.

www.sothebys.com   Site of the leading international auction house.

www.christies.com   Another leading auction house.

PORTFOLIO MONITORING

Risk assessment

www.riskmetrics.com   This is by far the most useful and important site for checking out your portfolio's risk characteristics and is provided by an offshoot of JP Morgan, the Wall Street investment bank. You load up your details and it comes up with a risk grade relating your portfolio risk to market risk. It also suggests changes in your portfolio to reduce risk and goes some way to quantifying your downside exposure. Works for UK and global shares, bonds and funds.

www.finportfolio.com   An excellent US site allows you to risk rate your portfolio and check out its overall risk characteristics.

www.thomsonfn.com   Has a number of tools to compare risk versus returns.

www.barra.com   An institutional site with a number of useful pages explaining risk.

www.efficientfrontier.com   An excellent educational oriented site on risk versus return.

www.wsharpe.com   Has the latest views of the Nobel Laureate and risk theorist, Bill Sharpe.

Insider trades

Monitoring trades by directors and officers of companies is popular in the USA where sites such as www.insiderscores.com rank directors on the success of their previous trades. www.thomsonfn.com also focuses on the trades of institutional investors, who are believed to be worth following because they are close to companies. No UK sites currently exist which track these trades so closely.

FINANCIAL NEWS

These sites provided by UK newspapers and magazines online need no introduction. For an interesting global perspective look at the sites of the *Wall Street Journal* (www.wsj.com), recognized as the prime source of financial information in the USA and the website of Barrons (www.barrons.com), a weekly digest of US stock market events. Local newspapers in each area often provide sharply focused coverage of local businesses, for example, the *Liverpool Echo and Daily Post* (www.liverpool.com) covers local transport businesses in the UK port of Liverpool, while the *San Francisco Chronicle* (www.sfgate.com) provides coverage for local software companies in San Francisco. The list below covers the major UK national newspapers. There are particularly good search engines on the *Financial Times* and *Guardian* sites.

www.economist.com
www.telegraph.co.uk
www.financialnews.co.uk
www.ft.com
www.newsunlimited.co.uk
www.investorschronicle.co.uk
www.investorsweek.co.uk
www.scotsman.com
www.sharesmagazine.com
www.thisismoney.com
www.the-times.co.uk

NEWSWIRES

www.afxexpress.com
www.bbc.com
www.bloomberg.co.uk
www.breakingviews.com
www.bridge.com
www.citywire.co.uk
www.cnnfn.com
www.moreover.com
www.reuters.com
www.digitallook.com

UK DATA AND MARKET PRICES

www.advfn.com
www.freequotes.co.uk
www.ftmarketwatch.com
www.iii.co.uk
www.moneyextra.com
www.proquote.net
www.sharepages.com
http://finance.yahoo.co.uk

Appendix: Voices from the bulletin boards

TIPSTERS

With an Infinite number of Monkeys, some are bound to come up trumps!!
Bri
Blackdog@blueyonder.co.uk
18-Oct-2000

We need an initial source of info about shares and tipsters are as good a way as any of bringing a share into the spotlight. This should obviously be followed up by your own research (DYOR) and price monitoring before buying. Sunday newspaper tips are the worst IMHO written by journalists and not analysts. Bulletin boards have their critics, but I am a big fan, especially when you find those with serious posters who can link you into other shares that you may not have considered. Stockbrokers, like travel agents and other intermediaries, must be getting a little worried by the power of the internet.
Matt Blacker
Youngan7@hotmail.com
5-Aug-2000

I would rather pay for a service which (like the professionals have in the City) gives me almost instantaneous info, refs, trades, prices, etc. This would allow me to make up my own mind about what action to take and would be especially attractive for active traders. For long-term traders, the City boys have already hit the price by X% (insert your own guess) before you can buy into the stock – so you have to hang on there a bit longer to realize a gain, with of course the danger that its only being ramped and that you might be sitting on a paper loss for some time.
jamie
grobuk@compuserve.com
20-Oct-2000

Naturally any sensible investor will pay a reasonable amount for quality tips. However, most are also Gardeners and they know that gardening advice tells them to put the plant in the shade but not the sun, put it into ventilation but not a draught, keep it damp but not wet. They also know that to do these things they must stand over the plant all day and do nothing else. Same with investment advice. In the end time, chance, contrary advice and every other variable makes you rely upon common sense and experience but proven, inexpensive and quick advice is always worth it if you can get it. That is also how you run a business.

Stan Kaiser
stan@kaisers.freeserve.co.uk
18-Oct-2000

After paying TW for access to his tips, I find each and every one has tanked. Wiggins, InterX and others are now way below what I paid. Hell, I bought InterX at £9 and then doubled up when it fell to £6 because of his recommendations. From now on I will Do My Own Research and not rely on other 'more experienced' people to do it for me. Next fun bit is telling the wife on Valentines Day that all our savings have gone:-(

Steve
bargainhunta@yahoo.co.uk
19-Feb-2001

I do not normally buy any shares recommended by anyone. The tips give me a lead to further my research. And then subsequently after thorough scrutiny of the companies I will then decide whether to buy or not. This is just pure common sense. Anyone who just buys on tips given is trading on dangerous grounds.

Robert Wong
bobbyw_lon@yahoo.com
12-Mar-2001

I would keep away from these analysts … they are nothing but bunch of glorified salesmen and retail investor are the last one to gain if lucky from their tips … once their clients and chumps have bought the shares. Just ignore this Kavanagh, Winnifrith etc etc donkeyholes!!!

A Norris
Norris@hotmail.com
11-Mar-2001

Thought for the day: If tipsters were any good at tipping, they would be
rich men instead of advisers to rich men (or should that now be 'poor'
men!)
Grister
brund@rampers.fsnet.co.uk
6-Mar-2001

The danger comes from treating these people as 'experts' and following
their recommendations slavishly. However, when combined with good
practice such as setting and activating stop-losses, they can be a useful
source of investment ideas – but only that! It is the investor's
responsibility to manage his/her portfolio properly. However, there is
great difference across the tipsheets and tipsters. Some are professional
and are frank about their mistakes; the other extreme are rampers who I
suspect to be on the criminal margin, i.e. ramping for self-gain. IMHO, of
course.
John Page
john@pagehome.demon.co.uk
26-Feb-2001

During the bull run in the market a child of 12 could have picked a string
of winners. Since then they have lived off those good times. However, the
tide has turned and they are now shown up as the charlatans they are. Let
this be a lesson to us all.
Crooked Tipsters
johnslade70@hotmail.com
19-Feb-2001

THE BUBBLE

An analyst is someone who is too bullish when a company is doing well,
and too bearish if the company does not reach their expectations.

Oldiron
s.lawrence25@cableinet.co.uk
2-Apr-2001

I feel really sorry for people who have lost money, with the so-called experts tips, I am very surprised that these guys did not tell you to sell and bail out shares like InterX, there was no sign of them going back up, I basically run a stop loss, and wait for some evidence of the shares going back up even if I pay more for them than what I sold them for. If a share goes down more than 25 per cent, there is something wrong, those guys know this, why did they not tell us? Strange!

Craig Wyper
wipo1@hotmail.com
6-Mar-2001

What really annoyed me was that if you opened an investment magazine last year about a hundred inserts imploring you to get 'Tip top profits from top tips' would fall out on the floor. Hopefully this collapsing market will see an end to this. Realistically, the same people attacking the tipsters are the same people who would have lost their shirts at Lloyd's Insurance. Read the small print!

GrimReaper
not_for_hire@yahoo.co.uk
21-Feb-2001

At the time the chiefs of BT were bidding for the G3 licences the share price was? (Around £12–15) If that were to be sustainable the company had to become global, almost at any cost. They had a tiger by its tail and could not let go, hence the overspend during the last twelve months?

A.Dyer
anthonydyer@btinternet.com
18-May-2001

Greed! I have worked within the internet arena and it is now clear that unless a business can reduce costs or improve revenue then it does not make sense to make a large investment. Old Economy Rules still make sense. However do not be pessimistic as good use of the internet can provide both of these benefits.

Oma
xxxttt@hotmail.com
7-Aug-2001

It is unbelievable to think that any company could be worth several billion pounds when its revenues for the year were less than 30 million and its losses were even more, and profits were years away. (Baltimore and all the other 90 per cent fallers). Get real people and invest in reality, not hype. Everyone is to blame, the hypers, the grabbers, the greedy.
Martin Lawlor
mj_lawlor@hotmail.com
7-Aug-2001

This is a classic example of people not being prepared to take responsibility for their own actions. If a stock went up it was the investors who claimed it was their brilliant choice and they deserved the rewards – if a stock went down the investors claimed they were badly advised and they wanted compensation.

Human nature – isn't it wonderful!
nick
6-Aug-2001

The bigger companies just take everyone else to the cleaners by manipulating the market with their comments and trading power. Having faster (mis) information just makes the problem worse as the private investors are likely to have a quicker reaction to the news in terms of buying and selling. Who knows – net companies might actually be worth something after all, but they're so volatile that no one can get a good valuation. Happy day trading!
Shifty
andrewclift@yahoo.com
6-Aug-2001

A wise trader would try to understand all methods of stock picking; for what is important to other market participants necessarily affects their decisions and therefore should by default be important to anyone who wants to understand why shares move the way they do.

Tom
t.jolly@index247.co.uk
11-Apr-2001

RISK

Risk is completely relative to the individual and their circumstances, therefore risk measurements could be very misleading if people don't interpret them properly.
Mike Embrey
payrme@hotmail.com
23-Apr-2001

If I'm walking along a cliff edge on a windy day, I know it's risky, it seems odd to try and put a figure on that, say 457, what?
Keith Beef
nicesprouts@hotmail.com
21-Apr-2001

On what basis are the risk judgments to be made? Empirical, analytical, evidential? A relative measure of risk is not a measure of total risk. Seems a useful but limited first step.
Gerald Rosenberg
g.rosenber@bris.ac.uk
20-Apr-2001

Well known 'fact' that no one admits to being a bad driver, bad lover or bad manager.
Honest Al
a.b@c.d
6-Jul-2001

TECHNICAL ANALYSIS

In a freely traded share or commodity price takes into account all known facts. So please do not confuse me with fundamentals.
sri
sri@srikaservices.freeserve.co.uk
5-Apr-2001

Following charts is for those who like playing with crayons rather than engaging in considered analysis. Of course, if we all did charts it would be a self-fulfilling prophecy … in the short term.
Nick Beart
4-Apr-2001

Every tipster/tip sheet has some hidden objective. You simply don't know whom to believe. Charts are impartial and work especially in a world of mass-market manipulation and market abuse. Long live the chartists.
richard scarlett
clusterfour@hotmail.com
3-Apr-2001

All Technical Analysts have 20/20 hindsight but not a Scooby Doo about the future – they'd be as well gutting a chicken and reading the entrails!
Tom Watson
piershill_777@hotmail.com
2-Apr-2001

Technical analysis is the only way to make logical decisions that can be back tested, on when to buy and when to sell. It works on any market and any timescale.

Mike Alexander
r231imex@msn.com
2-Apr-2001

TA is merely a consensus accepted by insiders. It does not follow any real flow being only supported by itself. It is a more complicated version of herd following.
F.C. Mole
frederick.mole@cwcom.net
18-Mar-2001

SHAREHOLDER DEMOCRACY

The big boys in the City have all the say at meetings. A couple of questions from the floor are taken normally from some shareholder who has bought in at a bad price. As the law stands, to get an EGM to stir things up you need 10 per cent of the shareholders to agree to get a meeting – very hard to get that amount. I have tried three times to do this and normally you can only get 4 to 7 per cent.
Ed Fits
edfit@edfits.co.uk

AT THE HEIGHT OF THE UK BUBBLE: FEBRUARY 2000

The price of Baltimore on Nasdaq at the moment is $177 which is about £118 if the share price is directly comparable. Like I suspect most investors only have a vague idea of what Baltimore does. However, internet security seems to be vital and more important it must be highly specialised and thus pose a significant barrier to entry insofar as competition is concerned. Last week the results showed an annual turnover of £23m and a market capitalisation of about £4bn which scared some investors. However, Freeserve's interims reported a turnover for 6 months of £7m and it has a capital value of nearly £8bn. Which company would you rather invest in? I agree with Mr Hutchison's wise words. Stop reading too much into some fluctuations and look at the bigger picture. This is a major company for the future and you will really kick yourself in a few years' time if you sell out now. I bought in at £48 when the price graph was pretty steep and I daresay similar discussions were taking place about whether or not the price was too high then. Sit tight, this company looks like a real winner.

AlyB 28/02/00, 21:13

Index